WHAT YOUR DREAMS ARE TELLING YOU

UNLOCKING SOLUTIONS WHILE YOU SLEEP

CINDY McGILL

WITH DAVID SLUKA

Chosen

a division of Baker Publishing Group
Minneapolis, Minnesota

Published by Chosen Books
11400 Hampshire Avenue South
Bloomington, Minnesota 55438
www.chosenbooks.com

Chosen Books is a division of
Baker Publishing Group, Grand Rapids, Michigan

Printed in the United States of America

Library of Congress Cataloging-in-Publication Data
McGill, Cindy.
    What your dreams are telling you : unlocking solutions while you sleep / Cindy McGill, with David Sluka.
        pages cm
    Includes bibliographical references.
    Summary: "Dreams can and do contain insight and answers into everyday problems. Here a dream expert gives you the tools to interpret these messages"—Provided by publisher.
    ISBN 978-0-8007-9565-8 (pbk. : alk. paper)
    1. Dreams. 2. Dream interpretation. I. Title.
BF1078.M368 2013
154.6'3—dc23   2013017682

Cover design by Yvonne Parks

To my husband, Tim, who has been so loving, supportive and encouraging as we have journeyed on this road of understanding dreams together.

To all of my dream teams, who have sacrificed unselfishly even in bitterly cold and uncomfortably hot temperatures, to give encouragement to dreamers all over the world.

To you, the reader—a dreamer. Whether you are just starting to connect with your dreams or have been aware of your dreams for years, may this portal of communication open wide for you so that you can hear the messages of encouragement to guide you on the path of truth, which will surely bring you more than you could ask, think or imagine.

CONTENTS

9. **How to Reawaken Your Dreams**

Many things get in the way of our dreams and try to shut
them down—our responsibilities, life's difficulties, other
voices in our lives. Sometimes we just forget them. It is time
for our dreams to come alive again.

10. **Dream On and Live**

Dreams are meant to give you hope toward something
better; they unlock a door for you to achieve your full
potential without hindrance. Your dreams are meant to
help you make the most of your life. You have a reason to
live, so dream on and dream big!

INTRODUCTION

I am a dreamer with a desire to help everyday people understand what their dreams are telling them. Over the years, the dream teams I have led have interpreted literally thousands of dreams. Our findings have been overwhelmingly educational as people have discovered the messages given to them in their dreams and have experienced life-changing results—improving and sometimes saving their lives.

I have also had my critics, who feel that my desire to understand more about dreams has been "controversial" or has come from a misguided perspective. My answer is, "You are not my audience." History has shown that dreams provide solutions for everyday success in business, science, education, government, arts and entertainment—wherever people live and work. I want to be a catalyst to help world changers understand and benefit from this portal of communication. My ultimate goal is to deliver encouragement and hope to others so that they live out their lives with purpose and strength.

When a person tells me a dream, I genuinely try to understand what the true meaning may be, regardless of my personal convictions. I encourage you to do the same with this book as you read about the inexhaustible and universal language of dreams. If you read with an open heart, not rushing through the content, I trust that these pages will broaden your understanding of the subject of dreams and will provide answers for your life's journey.

1

RESULTS WHEN YOU LISTEN

What kind of business results do you think a dream at night could inspire? How about a $4.4 billion increase in revenue! In 2004 Julie Gilbert Newrai was creating a new business called Magnolia Home Theater for Best Buy Company, Inc. As she built Magnolia, she continually asked herself if a frontline employee or a customer with the same idea as she had could ever realize the opportunity of bringing a new, game-changing business to life. With that in mind, she created an internal program inviting the creative voices of employees and customers to be heard. The passion and innovation she found in these voices deeply impacted Julie.

As part of the business development process, Julie also interviewed high-end male customers and their wives, which increased her awareness of the influence and spending power of women. Simply put, women were making the overwhelming majority of purchases in Best Buy stores (and in every major industry around the globe), and no process existed to bring their fresh ideas to life.

During this time, Julie had a dream taking her back to her childhood when she would stay up late at night listening to wolves howl.

She immediately saw the similarity between what was happening at Best Buy and the voices of the wolves. The voices of customers and customer-facing employees were like the howls, except that they went unheard and therefore were not receiving the attention necessary to bring forth any winning combination of business ideas.

Inspired by this dream, Julie created WOLF, which she defines as "a methodology and structure of global innovation teams." These teams, called wolf packs, were comprised of customers and employees. The wolf packs were connected to key executive business leaders who could implement the best ideas the wolf packs generated about training, marketing, call centers, website design, store design, hiring and other key business elements.

Four years after the dream that led to Julie's creation of WOLF, some of the business outcomes it achieved at Best Buy included:

- $4.4 billion increase in revenue from female customers (11 percent increase in total company revenue)
- Highest ever female market share in company history
- Largest increase in brand perception in company history
- Passionate, global, viral customer networks growing market share and innovating new business offerings
- 5 percent reduction in female turnover, resulting in a minimum of $25 million in savings
- 18 percent increase in the number of female employees
- 40 percent increase in female general managers and general managers in training, and 60 percent increase in female operations managers

In response to WOLF's success, numerous Fortune 100 businesses and nonprofits sought out Julie and her WOLF methodology for assistance in developing new products and services for the female market. In May 2009, Julie formed a consulting firm, WOLF Means Business, as a way to help numerous organizations authentically innovate and grow their businesses.

Julie's dream led to a solution—a mutually profitable solution for a company, its customers and its employees—that began with inviting unheard voices to make a difference. Because Julie responded to this dream in the night, Best Buy saw amazing results from 2004 to 2009. Since then, her award-winning work has spread to other businesses around the world through WOLF Means Business.[1]

Everyone Dreams Every Night

You have the same potential to see positive results by acting on the dreams you have at night. Often I hear people say, "Well, I don't dream at night." Research shows that except in a few cases of injury (and you are probably *not* one of those cases), *everyone has about four dreams each night.*[2] Those deprived of dreams actually become irritable, have difficulty concentrating and hallucinate. Even more significant, if you were deprived of both food and dreams, you would die sooner from a lack of dreams.[3]

You will spend about one-third of your life sleeping and have over 1,400 dreams each year.[4] That means by the time you are forty (about half of your life), you will have had over 56,000 dreams. About 80 percent of the time that babies are sleeping, they are dreaming. The rest of us dream about every 90 minutes that we are asleep throughout the night.[5] Unfortunately, within five minutes of waking up you usually forget half of your dream, and within ten minutes, 90 percent is gone.[6]

It is inaccurate, therefore, when people say, "I don't have dreams." More accurately, people who think they do not dream are just not remembering their dreams when they wake up. But this can be changed!

Dreams have captured our attention for thousands of years. The Jewish Bible records the first dream of Abraham, who lived between 2100 and 1800 BC.[7] The Chester Beatty Papyrus, written around 1350 BC, is the oldest dream dictionary in existence today. It describes special dream-interpreting priests called "Masters of the Secret Things" or "Learned Ones of the Magic Library."[8]

After the printing press was invented, a dream dictionary called *Oneirocritica* or *The Interpretation of Dreams* by second-century author Artemidorus Daldianus became one of the first bestsellers, comparable only to the Bible in popularity.[9] Fast-forward a few thousand years and search "dream facts" on the Internet, and you will find an overwhelming abundance of information about night dreams.

By the time we die, most of us will have spent a quarter of a century asleep, of which six years or more will have been spent dreaming. Sleep is so much more than just a time to rest your body. It is also a time to receive messages that can help you when you are awake. Why waste this time merely sleeping? Use it to receive the information you need to live a more successful, satisfied life!

The Inspiring Power of Dreams

Throughout history—for those who have listened—dreams have inspired inventions, scientific discoveries, businesses, books, songs and poetry. They have warned of danger and have provided insight and direction. It is time to pay attention to this extraordinary source of enlightenment—your dreams.

In the rest of this chapter, I want to tell you some amazing stories of how dreams have inspired and enlightened people. Let's start by taking a look at how dreams have led to many significant discoveries.

Sewing Machine

Elias Howe (1819–1867) was trying to build a machine that would automate the process of sewing. After numerous attempts and a great deal of frustration, he had a dream about being attacked by cannibals with spears. As the natives thrust their spears at him—back and forth, back and forth, back and forth—he noticed that their spears had a hole at the *tip*.

When he woke up from the dream, he realized that he should put the hole at the point of the needle, not at the backside of the needle, as he had been trying to do previously. He went to his shop, made some changes in his design and invented the sewing machine.[10]

Theory of Chemical Structure

In 1862 the German organic chemist Friedrich August von Kekulé dreamed of a snake biting its own tail. He said that this dream led to the discovery of the ring shape of the benzene molecule. His theory of chemical structure significantly advanced the development of chemistry.[11]

Discovery of Insulin

In 1920 Frederick Banting, an unknown Canadian surgeon who had an interest in diabetes, had a dream that led to one of the biggest discoveries in medicine. Unable to sleep one night during a time when he was preparing for a lecture, he woke up after a dream and wrote down brief instructions that would lead to the discovery of insulin and the treatment for diabetes. He was awarded the Nobel Prize in Physiology or Medicine for this discovery.[12]

Nerve Impulses

Otto Loewi was a German pharmacologist who has been referred to as the "Father of Neuroscience." In the early spring of 1923, he dreamed of an experiment with frogs that would show that the transmission of nerve impulses was chemical rather than electrical. He woke up after the dream and wrote down the idea, but in the morning he could not read his notes. He spent the entire day trying to reconstruct his dream. The following night he had the same dream, woke up and went to the lab to perform the experiment. This research led to a Nobel Prize in Physiology or Medicine in 1936.[13]

Australian John Eccles was another neuroscientist who won the Nobel Prize in Physiology or Medicine in 1963 for his work on the synapse. His Golgi cell theory, a key element of his work, originated in a dream. Eccles wrote in his memoirs,

> Then in 1947 I developed an electrical theory of synaptic inhibitory action which conformed with all the available experimental evidence. Incidentally this theory came to me in a dream. On awakening I remembered the near tragic loss of Loewi's dream so I kept myself awake for an hour or so going over every aspect of the dream, and found it fitted all experimental evidence.[14]

Periodic Table of the Elements

One night in February 1869, Dmitri Mendeleyev, a Russian scientist, had a dream of "a table where all the elements fell into place as required." This led to the first version of the Periodic Table of the Elements, which was foundational for modern chemistry.[15]

Optical Computers

While working for AT&T Bell Laboratories, Alan Huang had a recurring dream about computers in which "two bodies of data were marching towards each other like great armies. The two forces would come ever closer, but just as they were about to have a collision, Huang would wake up. The dream was a manifestation of a problem haunting Huang at work."[16]

One night after having the dream again, he did not wake up just before the collision but saw the bits of data in each army pass through each other without colliding. This dream led to optics replacing electronics inside computers, which was a major breakthrough in computers.[17]

Aren't you thankful that these people paid attention to their dreams, wrote them down and acted on them? We can all be thankful Banting wrote down his dream and followed the guidance provided to change the lives of millions of diabetics. Let's look at other dreams throughout history that have had a significant impact.

Victories and Defeats in War

Pompey dreamed of defeat, and Caesar's death was foretold in a dream.[18] Prior to invading Italy, Hannibal asked for a dream about his future military activities. He saw himself winning decisive victories and decided to persevere in his conquest of Italy.[19] Napoleon's defeat at Waterloo was foretold in a dream. The night before the battle, he dreamed that a large, black cat moved back and forth between his army and the opposition, eventually lying down with his French troops. The following day, the opposing armies unexpectedly defeated Napoleon's army.[20]

Sitting Bull's Victory at Little Big Horn

Before the battle of the Little Big Horn in 1876, Sitting Bull dreamed that soldiers were falling upside down from the sky like grasshoppers into the Indian camp. As they fell he heard a voice cry, "I give you these because they have no ears."

Sitting Bull took it as a sign that the battle would be won and prepared for war. He believed the soldiers were given up to him because they would not listen to the Great Spirit.[21]

Abraham Lincoln's Dream of His Murder

Abraham Lincoln had a lifelong interest in dreams and took them very seriously. A few days before John Wilkes Booth shot and killed him in Ford's Theater, Lincoln had a dream in which he saw a corpse wrapped in funeral clothes, lying in a casket. When

Lincoln asked in his dream, "Who is dead in the White House?" he was told, "The president. He was killed by an assassin!"[22]

What if Abraham Lincoln had had a dream interpreter available who had advised his security team to step up protection for him so that he was not in the wrong place at the wrong time? I wonder if his life would have been spared.

The Sinking of the Titanic

There were nineteen documented cases of dreams that predicted the sinking of the *Titanic*. The nineteen people who had these dreams included several passengers, some of whom paid attention to their dreams and survived, while others ignored them and drowned.[23]

St. Patrick's Escape from Slavery

St. Patrick was born in Britain about AD 390. He was kidnapped and sent as a slave to tend sheep in Ireland for six years. It is said that Patrick had a dream that showed him how to escape, which he did. He was then reunited with his family. His dreams also told him to return to Ireland and spend the rest of his life as a priest, which he did.[24]

Freedom for Slaves

Harriet Tubman had many vivid dreams that she believed were from God. She used them to guide hundreds of escaped slaves to freedom through the Underground Railroad.[25]

Famous Book Ideas

Robert Louis Stevenson came up with *Strange Case of Dr Jekyll and Mr Hyde* while he was dreaming.[26] Mary Shelley conceived of the story *Frankenstein* in a dream.[27]

The Nike Brand Name

In 1964 University of Oregon track coach Bill Bowerman, along with Phil Knight, a middle-distance runner, formed Blue Ribbon Sports. Jeff Johnson signed on in 1965 as the company's first full-time salesperson, and they opened the first Blue Ribbon Sports retail outlet the following year. According to Korky Vann's online article "Nike: From Greek Myth to Sports and Fitness Powerhouse,"

> In 1971, Johnson made an incalculable contribution to the company: One night, he dreamed of Nike, the Greek goddess of victory, and suggested the name to his bosses. The company used the moniker for its first footwear product to feature the "Swoosh" mark—a soccer cleat called the Nike, whose name beat out Knight's suggestion that they call it the Dimension 6.[28]

The Tune for "Yesterday" by Paul McCartney

The tune for the song "Yesterday" came to Paul McCartney in a dream. McCartney said,

> I woke up with a lovely tune in my head. I thought, "That's great, I wonder what that is?" There was an upright piano next to me, to the right of the bed by the window. I got out of bed, sat at the piano, found G, found F sharp minor 7th—and that leads you through then to B to E minor, and finally back to E. It all leads forward logically. I liked the melody a lot, but because I'd dreamed it, I couldn't believe I'd written it. I thought, "No, I've never written anything like this before." But I had the tune, which was the most magic thing![29]

According to the *Guinness Book of Records*, this song has the most cover versions of any song ever written. According to record label BMI, it was performed over seven million times in the twentieth century. That dream had some serious return on investment!

Unlock Your Future

What am I trying to say? Everyone dreams. *You* dream. Are you listening to your dreams? What are your dreams telling you?

At the start of each chapter that follows, I have included a short segment containing dreams other people have sent to me. Each segment demonstrates how a person's dream provided a solution to a situation that needed an answer.

Do you need some answers? It is time to wake up and pay attention to the messages you are receiving at night through your dreams. Those messages are your path to unlocking solutions for a better future.

TAKEAWAYS

- Throughout history, dreams have unlocked solutions in fields such as business, government, leadership, science, music, mathematics and literature.
- You dream about four dreams every night. That totals 1,460 dreams each year.
- Dreams can provide solutions while you sleep—if you will pay attention.

2

A JOURNEY INTO
DREAM INTERPRETATION

Situation: I was seeking creative ways to make money from home.

Dream: I was visiting a bead shop and found very pretty daisy beads, from which I made a bracelet. The dream was happy and joyful, and I woke up cheerful the next day.

Solution: I started making jewelry and took several classes to learn how to do it well. I just recently found the courage to sell several pieces and was pleasantly surprised at how fast they sold. It has been a process over several years, but I am now starting to receive some income from this business.

Dreams have not only been significant throughout history; dream themes are also everywhere today. They are on stationery, candles, books and bookmarks. Advertising slogans and themes are full of them, and so are movies such as *Premonition* with Sandra Bullock and *Inception* with Leonardo DiCaprio (which grossed $62.7 million the opening weekend). Dream websites abound, and prominent talk show hosts such as Dr. Phil and Oprah recognize dreams as a valid source of communication and have done shows featuring dream experts. *The Today Show, Good Morning America*, CNN, CBN and FoxNews have also highlighted dreams and dream interpretation.

A headline in a recent online article read, "Deathbed theory dreamt by an Indian maths genius is finally proved correct—almost 100 years after he died."[1] The article tells the story of renowned Indian mathematician Srinivasa Ramanujan, who claimed that this theory and other mathematical functions came to him in dreams. Researchers are saying his formula may explain the behavior of black holes.

Emory University mathematician Ken Ono was quoted in the article as saying, "No one was talking about black holes back in the 1920s when Ramanujan first came up with mock modular forms, and yet, his work may unlock secrets about them." Tragically, Ramanujan died at the age of thirty-two of tuberculosis, but the formulations in mathematics he received in dreams and rigorously pondered during his waking hours paved the way for many scholars who came after him.

We cannot deny that secrets are revealed in dreams. Not all dreams have significant meaning, but you will not be able to shake off those that need interpretation until you have an answer. Ramanujan spent so much time thinking about math that he flunked out of college in India two times. I am not suggesting that you approach your dreams with this level of intensity, but answers do come to those who listen to what their dreams are saying.

Growing into Dream Interpretation

As a child I remembered my dreams when I woke up, but I did not understand what they meant. When I was four or five years old, I began to dream about swimming fast under water for long distances without having to come up for air. I loved this dream! It was so much fun, and the dream recurred repeatedly until I was a teenager. It showed me that I was designed to explore the deep, hidden truths of life and enjoy it. I did not understand the meaning of this dream until I got older, but it clearly identified my natural design to explore mysteries, riddles and parables—things for which we have to seek answers.

Early on, I also started getting dreams about specific issues in my life and in the lives of others around me. When I would share a dream that pertained to another person, sure enough, that would be what was going on in his or her life. Sometimes I would get answers for the person about a certain situation. That is when I started to pay more attention to my dreams.

In about 1995, my husband, Tim, and I both started having dreams more vividly. Every night it was as though we were getting a major download of information about specific situations in our lives. One night we dreamed the same dream about flying, which put us on a path of seeing dreams as a valid and tangible way to receive information that would help us in life.

We started putting more weight on dreams as a source of communication and found out that we were able to unlock secrets and mysteries in our own lives and in the lives of others. Our dreams even began to expand in their influence as we purposed to make ourselves available to listen to and interpret other people's dreams.

A Crash Course in Interpretation

At the 2002 Winter Olympics in Salt Lake City, Utah, a number of people we knew who were learning to interpret dreams were invited to be part of a "dream team" we hosted during the Olympic Games. Our goal was to get out and see what people were dreaming and

25

to provide them with dream interpretations. In previous years, I had learned a bit about dream interpretation and had started to practice what I had learned.

One evening, one of our team leaders was invited to a private party in Park City, Utah, and I was left in charge of the whole team. We had made arrangements to take a dream team to a bar in downtown Salt Lake. The bar had advertised that we would be there to do free dream interpretation.

I was nervous because I did not feel confident in my own ability to interpret dreams. To lead a team to interpret on a larger scale was an even greater stretch for me. But I decided that we would go anyway and see what happened. When we told people that we were practicing dream interpretation, they were more than willing to help us out by telling us their dreams.

I went into the bar and met two girls who were sisters. One girl had a dream—not an easy dream, in my opinion. The dream was very detailed, and I had to listen closely to her description of it. As I listened, I saw a picture unfold in my mind. The dream was being put together like a puzzle for me. I wrote down what I saw on a piece of paper, and when she finished, I shared the few words that were highlighted to me. Soon the girl was crying. It was a dream providing direction for her life, and it unraveled a mystery for her. Authentic dream interpretation will unravel mysteries and unlock doors; it will reveal or give insight into something that was unseen before.

Our whole team walked away from that experience more confident. The major lesson we learned was that every person and every dream encounter is different. Some dreams will be life changing, and some will not have a deep meaning. Those dreams are simply visions passing through our heads at night as we are processing life. But when a dream is given to provide meaningful direction, you do not want to miss the chance to take full advantage of the hope and guidance being offered.

Interpretation at the Park

On Sunday afternoons, a few of us started to set up dream interpretation signs at a nearby park. Fifty to seventy-five drummers from the area would bring their djembes, congas and other percussion instruments to the park, and they would hang out, picnic and play music. We became part of their "tribe."

Our team wanted to bring answers to people who had perplexing dream messages, but we understood that a bridge of communication had to be built so that these dreamers would trust us with their dreams. We used a menu board to display our "services offered," and our menu items spoke directly to people's needs. They would pick from the menu whatever they felt they had need of. People began to talk to us, and we would interpret their dreams. We became quite popular, and everyone looked forward to seeing us each week. We got practice, and they got helpful information about their lives.

We found that dream interpretation was a highly effective way to engage this group of people at the park because they had questions and needed answers for what they were experiencing in life. They did not know where to go for answers, but they had mysterious dreams and we could bring understanding to those mysteries.

Taking It on the Road

From there we went to an expo in Spokane, Washington, where we offered dream interpretation out of a tent. Our tent became so popular that we were quadruple-booked for each fifteen-minute time slot, which forced us to call in more people to expand our team.

As we saw the need and realized how much interest people had in dreams and their interpretation, we began to bring teams to the Sundance Film Festival and capture dream interpretation on film. We met numerous producers and people in the movie industry and learned that many movies come from dreams people have. We continue to send teams to that festival each year. Sometimes we have had forty dream interpreters on the streets at Sundance or other festivals, just walking around and striking up conversations with people about their dreams. Once people found out about us, we had so many people wanting to tell us their dreams that we could not get to them all. Forty dream interpreters were not enough to meet the demand.

When we did call-in programs offering dream interpretations on the radio, the DJ would tell us that the phones were still lighting up long after we left the studio. Dreamers know when they are getting an accurate interpretation, and they hunger for more. Wherever we went, we found people who were seeking solutions to their problems. People who were having dreams about specific situations in their lives would receive an interpretation that gave direction, which would enable them to avoid making a significant personal or professional mistake. These people were so thrilled with the guidance they received that they freely gave us their business cards and offered their support for whatever we did. They followed us and called friends they knew who had dreams, and their friends got their dreams interpreted as well.

In 2004 I went to the Burning Man festival for the first time. It takes place in the Black Rock Desert of Nevada and is a ten-day festival of creative artists who create communities of free expression. These communities are full of spiritual seekers. The attendance reaches over fifty thousand people, all coming together within a seven-mile radius. To meet the needs of the spiritual seekers, we set up a dream tent at Burning Man with a menu board displaying our "services," which included dream interpretation. The lines to have dreams interpreted were once again long because of the messages people were receiving in their dreams.

As of this book's printing, I have attended Burning Man festival eight more times. It is an incredible opportunity to meet people from all walks of life. Whether I am at Burning Man or anywhere else, I always find people who are longing to understand the mysterious language of night dreams.

In 2009 we filmed *Dreams: A Documentary*, which chronicled live dream interpretation encounters that took place at the Sundance Film Festival at Park City, Utah, that year. The response to the documentary has been very favorable. We make dream teams available after showings of the documentary so that those in attendance can have their dreams interpreted. One time, people were so impacted that they stayed past closing time and we had to be ushered out of the building.

One of my favorite places to interpret dreams is at a dream party. Someone will gather friends or business acquaintances who want some insight for their professional or personal lives. The dream party is usually held at someone's home, so the atmosphere is low-key and relational. Everyone walks away feeling hopeful. Some people have been so blown away with the information they received from an interpretation that they have made immediate changes in their lives or businesses. The dream interpretation caused them to go forward and be more profitable, whereas without it they might have taken a fall.

Making the Most of the Messages

People are receiving life messages in their dreams, and many times they cannot rest until those messages have been unlocked so that they can take action. When people have dreams that they know are of major importance, they begin a search to find someone who can offer insight and instruction. Because they know the message is important, their quest will continue until the correct interpretation of their dream is given.

All of my training and all of these experiences along my dream journey have proven to me beyond any doubt that dreams are a significant source of help to us. They help us be the best that we can be and make the most of our lives.

My history with dreams and dream interpretation has formed a framework that I use to interpret dreams. Let's look at that framework next.

TAKEAWAYS

- Dreams are a resource that can help you unlock answers for the questions you have.
- You have your own unique journey to take toward understanding what your dreams are telling you. Will you take it?

3

A FRAMEWORK FOR PROPER DREAM INTERPRETATION

Situation: I thought everything was okay with my other children after the birth of our new baby.

Dream: Our middle child (a three-year-old) was choking on nickels and dimes. My mother-in-law brought it to my attention, and I was able to reach into the child's mouth and get the change out of her throat so she could breathe again.

Solution: I took this dream as a warning telling us that we needed to reassure our three-year-old of our love for her so that she did not feel suffocated by the "change" of the new baby.

Most people create their own framework when they put their mind into dream-interpretation mode. The basic hindrance to proper interpretation is overinterpretation—trying to make the dream say something it is not saying. This happens when we misinterpret a symbol in the dream, or when our personal desires or concerns overtake the pure message of the dream.

Someone once told me a dream in which he saw bears in a forest being killed, loaded up on trucks and then taken out of the forest to be eaten. He started interpreting this dream by thinking it was about Russia because a bear is a well-known symbol for Russia. However, the right interpretation for this person was that the "bear" in his life was being killed, loaded up and taken out. This dream was saying that this person was going to overcome and "eat" (draw strength from) what had previously been a devouring force. What would have mistakenly been an impersonal, political interpretation very quickly became a personal encouragement to this dreamer.

Often when I am with a group of people who want their dreams interpreted, one person will hold back and have his or her friends go first. I once met three girls in their late teens who were excited about having us interpret their dreams. Two of the girls went first, but the third one had *the* dream—the one I knew would have the most significant impact on its dreamer. Because of her background and mindset, however, she was afraid that her dream might have a bad meaning, so she was checking us out to see what kind of information we were going to give her friends. After seeing that her friends' dreams had good interpretations, she entrusted her dream to us. The dream and its interpretation touched a very deep place within, and she received help for the situation she was in.

Dreams do require the proper mindset for proper interpretation. A strong, unreasonably strict upbringing can spin any message in a negative light. Some people live with subtle echoes—others with blatant messages—from a parent, schoolteacher, friend or neighbor who made them feel worthless. It is easy to think the worst about yourself with this type of background. We have all encountered negative emotions, but if you have encountered a great deal of rejection, fear and other emotional trauma in your life, you will naturally lean toward interpreting your dreams through the lens of life's hurtful experiences. A mindset of fear shuts down your ability to hear. A negative past does not promote a positive outlook on the future. However, if you view life knowing that there is hope for you, that you do not have to live your life in defeat and that you can learn to find light in dark places, then this lens will color your dreams in the right direction.

Dreams are designed to help you on your life's journey. If you can understand what you are designed to do, even in part, you can achieve what seems impossible. A dream, properly interpreted, gives hope and strength and will propel you into your destiny by opening doors that await you.

Seven Guides for Interpretation

To help beginning bowlers, bowling alleys often put down gutter bumpers on both sides of the lane. The bumpers keep the ball from going into the gutters, since that is where it tends to go most of the time for beginners. This chapter is all about setting in place some "bumpers," or a framework that will keep your dream interpretations on the right track. With this in mind, let's look at seven principles to consider as you explore your dreams.

1. Dreams Are for Your Good

A girl I met in New York had a dream that she was in a forest surrounded by eyeballs that were staring at her through the trees. She felt fear and anxiety in that situation. The interpretation I shared with her was that she was at a transition point in her life. She felt trapped because she could not "see the forest for the trees," so to speak. She did not know how to proceed to get out of the overwhelming circumstances that were blocking her path and her vision.

The eyeballs represented those who were watching and waiting for her to come out into the open and step into what she was made for. She would have great influence when she made her way out of the seemingly overshadowing circumstances that were blocking her in. The action she needed to take was to keep moving forward even though she could not see a clear path. In moving forward, she would find that facing the very obstacles that were hindering her would produce tenacity and endurance. On the other side she would find strength and courage, which she would not have gained without going through that transitional experience.

After I told this girl my interpretation of her dream, she then told me the interpretation she had received previously from another person. In response to her dream, this person instructed her to sit in a dark bathroom, in the bathtub, with crystals all around her to absorb the dark energy the dream supposedly signified. Thankfully, that interpreter did not bother to give her direction for her life, which is what she was looking for. The main reason people have their dreams interpreted is to find out the message and how to apply it to make life better. I do not think that interpreter's direction would have been very helpful.

As you approach dream interpretation, the first thing to remember is that dreams can be used for your good. If you have a history of nightmares, I am not suggesting a masochistic approach toward terrors of the night. We will talk more about where dreams come from in a few chapters, and people do experience dreams from dark, lying sources. However, as a general principle, dreams are to help you go forward into the future rather than hold you back. Dreams can give you another stepping-stone across the brook of life. Dreams can provide direction and keep you from trouble. Dreams can help you move past wrong thought patterns and a wrong identity and sense of self. Even dreams about falling or being chased speak the message that you have a future and something is trying to hinder it.

Dreams unlock hidden treasures—hidden truths that lead to greater wisdom and understanding. Dreams provide information to help you overcome difficulties, habit patterns, obstacles, ways of thinking, negative experiences, bad influences and generational waste that has been passed down to you. A dream can take off the chains and remove what is keeping you trapped. This is good news!

I once talked with a chef who was opening a restaurant in New York. He had dreams that sharks were chasing him in a tank, and he would wake up just before the sharks were going to eat him. In the dream, there was also a ceiling over the tank so he could not get out. It would have been easy to let that dream discourage him and assume it was foretelling defeat, especially given the success rate of opening restaurants in New York. However, the purpose of the dream was to give him the strength to overcome obstacles. Through this dream, he understood that the very thing he felt was chasing him actually was making him stronger, and soon the lid was going to come off. This chef is the type of person who is resilient, busts barriers, does not go with the status quo and has to be in things over his head in order to learn. It can be uncomfortable, but that is what makes him great. The "sharks" in this dream were actually driving him into his destiny and bringing him face-to-face with his fears in order to advance him into his future. After we talked about his dream, his response was, "That's amazing! Who needs Dr. Phil?"

Approach your dreams with confidence, knowing that dreams are meant to give you hope toward something better—to open a door and bring freedom from wrong thinking. Dreams can help you be the best you can possibly be. They can help you move into the place of full potential without hindrance. But you must move past negative processes, words and life experiences so you can interpret your dreams through a proper, clean lens.

Having this viewpoint about your dreams will give you vision to see yourself going for it and making the most of your life. It will bring hope to hopeless areas and a new beginning to what you thought was a dead end. Value your dreams. Do not just dismiss them when you wake up. Make them a priority because they can be really, really good for you.

2. Dreams Are Personal

Your dreams are mostly about you. That is why you have the dreams you do. Your dreams come in a language you can understand and in a way that is meaningful to you—if you pay attention and become familiar with your dream language. Someone close to you could have the same dream and it would not have the same impact because of the way it is given and personalized. You will become more familiar with your dream language as you read this book, apply its principles and see what your different dream themes mean for you.

Dreams contain a personalized message for you, and how you apply the message to your life must be personalized, too. In order for a dream to have an impact, you must own the message you have been given. Many people reason away experiences like dreams, but that does not mean they do not exist or do not have important meaning. Native Americans and other indigenous peoples around the world have understood the value and importance of dreams and have used the information to avoid pitfalls they face every day. I am of Cherokee descent, and as I have researched some of my own heritage, I have found this to be true.

While some people do have dreams that are broader in scope and go beyond themselves in application, it is best to start seeking out what your dreams mean to you personally before trying to apply them to another person or to a group of people.

Dreams are also contextual. Symbols in dreams should be applied to the whole dream to make a picture, like putting together a puzzle. That is why dream symbol books alone cannot give you the full interpretation of a dream. People have asked me questions like, "What does a swimming pool mean in my dream?" Trying to answer that kind of question is like someone handing you a blue puzzle piece and asking you to give insight on that piece. A blue puzzle piece in a picture can be the sky, water or any number of blue objects. Likewise, swimming pools can have different meanings in different dreams. Because dreams are personal and are customized just for you, it would be to your disadvantage to buy a dream symbol book and use *only* that to come up with a complete interpretation.

3. Dreams Are Often Parables with Symbols

Dreams are a picture language. Whatever a dream's meaning, one thing is for sure—picture language is unforgettable. The oldest records we have of dreams include symbols representing events that came to pass. One of the early rulers of Egypt had a dream that seven sick cows ate seven healthy cows, which was translated to mean that seven years of famine would follow and devour seven years of plenty. Even though the main symbol in the dream was a cow, the dream was not about cows. It was a warning dream to prepare a leader for what his country would face in the future.

In the same way, the main element or symbol in your dream may not define what the dream is about. Although some dreams are literal, they are mostly parables or pictures that illustrate a message you are supposed to hear. If you can remember the first two guides to interpretation—that *dreams are for your good* and that *dreams are personal*—you will be able to discern a dream's main message more clearly without complicating the meaning by trying to figure out all the complex symbols.

In the next chapter, we will explore in more detail the language, symbols and themes commonly found in dreams. I have also included a dream symbols appendix at the back of this book. But again, it is important *not* to interpret a dream by the symbols alone. I will talk more about that in the chapters ahead.

4. *Timing Is Important*

In thinking about past dreams, ask yourself, *When did I have this dream, and how many times have I had it?* The dreams you have had this week are relevant for today. There is a reason for the timing of your dreams—why you are having a certain dream now or why you had it at a certain time in the past.

In *Dreams: A Documentary*, my film that I mentioned putting together at the 2009 Sundance Film Festival, I share an encounter I had with a guy who was into the Gothic lifestyle. His dream was about being on a boat with friends. The boat took them to a deserted island, and they all got off the boat and played around for a while. Then all of his friends got back on the boat and sailed away, leaving him on the island alone with unseen forces that wanted to chase him and kill him.

Instantly a thought came to me when I heard that: *suicide*. I asked this young guy, "How long have you been suicidal?" He gasped, and all of his friends standing around listening gasped, too. Then I said, "You're not supposed to die early. This dream has been sent to help you so that your life is not a tragedy." The dream was also showing him that in isolation, he was a sitting duck, so to speak, for negative and unreasonable thoughts to try to direct his life.

Some people dream about events before they happen. Such dreams can include world events such as earthquakes, tsunamis and terrorist attacks. It is important to pay attention to keys within such dreams that point to the proper timing of their interpretation. After 9/11, I learned of many, many people who had dreamed of this event, but who did not think that it was literal. I have also received reports of dreams people had about the tsunamis in Indonesia and Japan.

A friend of mine from Belarus recently had a dream of a city here in the United States that was being governed under martial law because of a natural disaster. He told me it reminded him of the old Soviet Union. Lately people who do not know each other have been sending me dreams of an earthquake on the West Coast of the United States. Other disasters people have dreamed of include nuclear attacks and accounts of people running as fire is chasing them in big cities. Given the times in which we now live, it is important to pay attention to the timing of such dreams since they could be foretelling a literal event.

I have also received reports of people's dreams foretelling the acquisition of great wealth and lands, or dreams that have shown companies exploding with growth. A Facebook friend sent me the following message about a dream that described future events:

> I was having pain and was seeing a doctor for tests. All my tests came back as thyroid cancer, and I had surgery. The doctor told me that the cancer was the size of a pebble and that it was contained. While I was home recovering from surgery, I was reading through my dream journal and ran across this dream from about six months before the surgery: "I was in a doctor's office, and the doctor was Hawkeye Pierce from the TV show *M*A*S*H*. In the dream, he was looking down my throat. After a bit, he asked his nurse if she could see what he was seeing. She did, and the doc's advice was to have it taken out." The dream had foretold the situation with my throat and that it would take a "hawkeye" to see the small growth and remove it.

5. Dreams Come from Different Sources

Dreams can come from whatever you are around throughout the day—friends or other influences, work or your home environment, the media. In chapter 6 we will talk about three main sources of dreams: Self, Lie and Truth. The "voice" of these three often sounds the same, so we have to learn to follow the right one, which is the voice of Truth.

While not every dream is from Truth, I believe that God made every dreamer. He will guide you into truth if you will connect with Him for the interpretation of a dream. The key principle here is not to assume that every dream is leading you in the right direction, but to use discernment as you interpret your dreams.

6. *Do Something with Your Dreams*

Proper interpretation of your dreams can have incredible results. Taking action on a direction dream can launch you into a positive outcome for yourself, your family, your business, your employees, your co-workers and those around you. Invention dreams can prove to be a great resource for information that will prosper you and your business.

Everyone dreams, and each person must decide what he or she will do with the dreams that come. If you choose to use the information you have been given, you can move forward toward a positive outcome. If you do not use the information, then the outcome will be uncertain.

You are responsible for the information you receive through a dream and how you apply that information to your life. We will talk more about specific responses to dreams in the coming chapters, but the key is to put the information you receive in dreams to good use so it can benefit you in a good way.

7. *Connect the Dream with the Giver of Dreams*

If your car breaks down, you do not take it to a bakery or a shoe repair shop; you take it to a mechanic who can repair it properly. A mechanic knows how to make your car work according to its original design. In the same way, if we have things that are not working properly in our lives, the best option is to take our brokenness to the Creator who put us together. Then we can better understand how things work and why, how to get back on the right track and how to remain in true freedom, happiness and success. Let's face it—we all experience what I call "life trauma." There are things in all our lives that need fixing and healing.

You may have heard of the story of Job told in the Jewish, Muslim and Christian traditions—a man known for having experienced extreme suffering. The Bible records the following words of Job:

> For God does speak—now one way, now another—
> though no one perceives it.
> In a dream, in a vision of the night,
> when deep sleep falls on people
> as they slumber in their beds,
> he may speak in their ears
> and terrify them with warnings,
> to turn them from wrongdoing
> and keep them from pride,
> to preserve them from the pit,
> their lives from perishing by the sword.
>
> Job 33:14–18 NIV

Job clearly saw God as one who often gives people dreams for their own good. Think back to chapter 1 for a moment—about all the good that dreams have done through the centuries. I am sure some of those people we talked about may have connected their dreams to the Giver of dreams. But everyone dreams, so how many more inventions, medicines, discoveries and victories could have made history had more people listened to their dreams and to the Giver of those dreams?

Maybe you do not believe in God. That is okay. I interpret dreams for people of all faiths and for people with no faith. I also run into people who are very religious but think dreams are a thing of the past that should not be trusted today. Regardless of your spiritual beliefs, you will still have about four dreams tonight, and tomorrow night, and the next night and every night for the rest of your life. I encourage you to keep reading to learn what your dreams are telling you. My point here, though, is that if you will connect the gift of dreams with the Giver of dreams, I believe your gift will work much better.

Start with the Right Framework

It is important to step into dream interpretation with the proper framework. This means keeping in mind the seven principles for dream interpretation that I just covered. Value your dreams because they can be for your good. Remember that dreams contain personal messages for you that often come with symbols you will need to learn to understand. Consider the timing of your dreams. Why are you dreaming about a certain thing right now? Remember that dreams come from different sources—Self, Lie and Truth—so remember to use care and wisdom with your interpretation. Respond to your dreams in some way. The more you respond, the more your dreams will become a resource for guidance, hope and strength. And lastly, connect with the Dream Giver and the voice of Truth to guide you into all truth.

Next, let's look at the most common dream themes and symbols I encounter when I talk with people about their dreams.

TAKEAWAYS

- Have a proper framework in place as you consider what your dreams are telling you.
- Value your dreams, take a deeper look at them and begin to respond to them in some way.

4

COMMON DREAM THEMES

Situation: Our nine-year-old had a habit of taking on responsibilities that were either not her own or too much for her age, causing her to crash emotionally and physically.

Dream: She had a dream about being on a large motorcycle (she is very petite), crashing and then riding an age-appropriate scooter to get back home.

Solution: This dream helped us as parents have a meaningful conversation about this issue with our daughter. The dream showed her a picture of the effects of her choices, and it continues to be a helpful caution and encouragement to her to make sure that her responsibilities are manageable and ultimately lead her home.

Because each of us is unique, dream interpretations vary based on the person. One person may have a dream about a dog in which that dog represents a loyal friend. However, if a person was attacked by a dog in his or her past and is afraid of them, a dog in a dream may be a symbol of attack or violence. While the object, a dog, is the same for both people, the interpretations may be the exact opposite of each other. Dreams are mostly personal. They are based on the dreamer and what is going on in his or her life. The dreamer and the dream will fit together.

In this chapter we will look at dream themes people share with me most often. Each theme is divided into three parts: the meaning of the dream, questions to ask yourself (or the person who had the dream) and a suggested action to take in response. Dreams with the themes we will look at do not always have the meaning or application I mention (I run into exceptions every once in a while), but often they do.

These dream types are just a starting place—inspiration to help you search out and develop your own dream language. As you read, remember that dreams are to give you hope toward something better; they are an open door to unlock your full potential without hindrance. Your dreams are meant to help you be the best you can be and make the most of your life.

Teeth Falling Out

Meaning

This is probably the most common dream we run across while interpreting dreams on the streets. Most people instantly think they have dental problems, but let's look a bit deeper.

Think about what would happen if your teeth were really gone. You would be in danger of swallowing something whole. My grand-dad often used the phrase, "Let me chew on that for a while." I can understand now why he would say that. The longer you chew on food, the more flavor you absorb and the more time you have to decide if it is something you really want to "swallow." The food also goes down easier to give your body fuel. The same was true about whatever information my granddad was chewing on that might have applied to his life somehow.

This kind of dream is telling you that you are about to "swallow

44

something whole" because you are not able to break down the details (coinciding with the symbol that your teeth break down the food that affects your whole body). You may be losing your ability to understand something.

Questions to Ask

When did you have this dream? Why are you having this dream now? These dreams generally have something to do with what is going on in your life at the time that you have them. If this is a recent dream, then it applies now. If the dream occurred in the past, it applied to the circumstances that were happening at that time.

Suggested Action

This dream is a warning to get the details. If you are in a decision-making process right now—signing contracts, changing jobs, moving locations—get the details and do not be caught unaware. The general manager of an innovative manufacturing company in the power sports industry told me that at a time when he and his wife were in the middle of making a number of major decisions, he had a dream about his teeth falling out. His house was on the market, and he was considering a job change. This dream was a call for him to seek out more information and not move forward without getting the details.

Take stock of your life and the decisions you have made, and take time to pay attention. Be careful that you are not falling for something you have not examined carefully. In other words, as my granddad used to say, chew on it for a while.

Flying or Swimming Underwater

Meaning

Often a person who has flying dreams is very discerning, spiritually intuitive or insightful and can see things from a higher place or from a different perspective. This person generally has a free spirit, is not bound by circumstances, does not follow established rules and chooses to live above the situation.

Flying dreams have existed since ancient times, even before the invention of airplanes.[1] Flying or swimming dreams can mean that you are able to explore "higher" things or "deep" things not perceived by others, and this exploration is effortless for you. Your ability to catch the wind or the current brings you a sense of joy and release. Swimming underwater dreams can show your love to go deeper than the surface issues of life. Swimming underwater can also mean that you are involved in something over your head, or that you are designed to be in situations over your head.

These dreams have to do with freedom, soaring and living a life unhindered by anything. You may have the same flying or swimming dream a number of times. The message has something to do with who you are and what you have done or are doing.

The advantage is that if you are flying, you can definitely see things more clearly than if you are on the ground. And if you are deep in water, you can move around unnoticed and unhindered and see hidden things. Whether flying or swimming, this kind of dream shows that you come alive when you engage in that activity.

Questions to Ask

When I interpret a dream like this, I first ask, *Tell me about yourself (or about the person who had this dream)*. A person with flying or swimming dreams often has some or all of these qualities: artistic, thinks and lives out of the box, not fearful, has a unique perspective, overcomes difficult situations and comes alive in settings that allow for self-expression.

Where are you flying or swimming? The location can show where you come alive; for example, if you have a gift of teaching, you may dream about flying in educational institutions. Or the location can show the size or depth of your influence or pursuits; for example, it says something if you are swimming in an ocean versus a swimming pool or bathtub.

How often have you had the dream and for how many years? The number of times or how long you have had this dream (perhaps since you were a child) may show a key part of your identity and that you are being awakened to a gift resident inside of you.

Suggested Action

Accept your uniqueness and ability to see life from a different perspective. Contribute your point of view and make a difference. Search out the areas where you come alive and spend more time doing those things.

For example, a good friend has had multiple and ongoing dreams about flying in educational venues. As a person with a teaching gift, he comes alive in academic settings, and he tries to take opportunities to instruct and mentor others whenever possible.

When you are flying, you have unhindered access or limited opposition to where you want to go. Pursue going deeper into the issues of life. Have fun and go for it!

Falling

Meaning

No, this falling dream does not mean you are clumsy. It can often mean that you are a risk taker or are in a position where you must take a risk. Falling dreams often come to those who feel they must be in control. The need to be in control is not necessarily a bad thing; the dream can simply mean that your circumstances are just out of *your* control.

Usually, you are getting ready to enter into something new that you have not done before. If you are in a significant relationship, it can mean that you are "falling head over heels" for someone emotionally, or that the relationship is taking you in a direction that you were not expecting to go in. The dream can also apply to a job or a new situation that you are uncertain about, revealing that you do not know what to do.

When people are pushed into situations they did not see themselves getting into, they often will have falling dreams. This type of dream can also reveal life patterns of insecurity.

The main message to take away from falling dreams is that you are going to land where you are supposed to, even though things may appear out of your control. Remember that baby eagles do not learn to use their wings until their feet are off the ground and they are falling. The end result will be good, but you will have to trust. The course of your life may be shifting, and it will be different from what you thought.

I have heard people say that if you hit the ground during a falling dream, you will literally die in your sleep. I have fallen in my dreams and have hit the ground more than once and I am still here, so that myth has been proven untrue in my life. Do not worry—it is likely untrue in yours, too.

Questions to Ask

What is happening right now that you cannot control? Are there circumstances that have pushed you off a cliff, or do you find yourself in places or situations that you did not sign up for? Is your confidence low about who you are, or are you experiencing strong feelings of insecurity?

Suggested Action

Begin to explore and discover something brand-new. An open door is present for a new adventure. Take this opportunity to relinquish control and begin to trust. Do not become discouraged or hopeless. Look for the positive in your situation. Embrace who you are and the strengths you have been given. Move out of a place of insecurity, and move into who you are supposed to be.

Being Chased

Meaning

Something from your past is trying to affect your future, or there is something coming at you from behind to keep you from living up to your full potential. This can include anything that you are trying to overcome, such as past trauma, betrayal, fear, addiction, relationships or thought processes. Like the chef's shark dream I shared earlier, dreams about being chased can help you grow stronger in a certain area or break free from what is hindering your purpose in life—who you are made to be and what you are supposed to do. Whatever may be after you in your dream could very well be "chasing" you into your full potential so that you will not stagnate and settle for something less than what you are designed for.

Questions to Ask

How many times have you had the being chased dream? What are you trying to get away from or overcome? These dreams are usually recurring. The number of times you have had the dream can indicate the intensity of what you are trying to overcome. The frequency can also show how important it is that you persevere through every obstacle.

Suggested Action

Turn and face whatever is chasing you. Tell it firmly, "You will not hinder me any more! You no longer have a hold on me!" Remember that you are getting stronger in this area and do not give in. This thing is from the past, and that is why it is coming at you from behind.

Freedom is coming if you continue to move forward. Focus on the future and not the past. You may also want to look at where you are going when you are being chased. If you are headed toward healthy places of safety, this is showing a healthy response to whatever you are trying to overcome at this time. Be encouraged!

Naked in Public

Meaning

How fun is this dream? Everyone loves having the naked in public dreams, right? Come out from whatever you are scrambling to hide behind—nobody is looking at you like that. This dream may just be telling you that you are probably a person who is open and transparent, easy to read, and that "what you see is what you get." You are not hiding anything. Also note that this kind of dream is not sensual or sexual.

A dream about being naked in public may have to do with a situation you are facing. For example, if *you* are naked in your place of business, this dream may be showing that you feel vulnerable, uncovered or unprotected in some way at work. If your *co-workers* are naked, this dream may be showing that you have the ability to see beyond surface issues and perceive the heart of a matter.

This type of dream often has to do with integrity issues and may mean that you or someone else is about to be exposed. If you are okay with whatever situation you are in and you have nothing to hide, the situation will probably work out in your favor.

Questions to Ask

In what setting does this dream take place? Are you naked at work, at school, at home or around a group of friends? Do you recognize anyone in the dream? The location you are in tells you where you are vulnerable. The context is important. Whoever is looking at you tells you who the key people will be as this situation unfolds.

Suggested Action

Pay attention. This could be a warning dream that you need to come out with the truth before you are exposed in another manner. Get the information into the right hands before it becomes a mess. I often wonder if people who have been publicly exposed for indiscretions had naked in public dreams first as a warning to come clean.

If you have considered your integrity and your conscience is at rest, take consolation in the fact that you have nothing to hide, regardless of how things look. Know that in time, the truth about a situation will come out and you will be vindicated.

In the Bathroom

Meaning

Dreams about taking a shower, taking a bath or using the toilet show that a personal cleansing is taking place. You are being relieved of something or getting rid of it. Something is being removed that is unwanted or unneeded. If others are around or are watching you, then they are those who will observe what is happening in your life.

People have told us dreams where they are looking for a toilet because they have to use it so badly, but all of the toilets are full and overflowing. How frustrating! This kind of dream can show that a person has an urgent need to find relief from something and that it is all happening at once. Timing is important in this dream. I have found that when people are dreaming this kind of dream, they are usually in a pressing situation. The dream causes them to keep going to find a solution.

These in the bathroom dreams can also help us get rid of things that need to be cleansed and eliminated. All of us brush up against the impurities of this world, and the dream can be flushing it from your system. If you are in a negative atmosphere, this type of dream can help you release what you cannot naturally process while you are awake.

Your spirit is more perceptive than your physical senses. The things that happen during the day affect you mentally and emotionally and leave an imprint on your spirit. Dreams bring that imprint or image to life in the night season to help you gain a perspective you could never gain on a conscious level while awake.

Questions

Who is in the dream with you? That person or those people are there for a reason. For example, if you are on the toilet in front of all your co-workers, this dream applies to your workplace. If you are taking a shower at home and members of your family walk in, you may be going through personal cleansing at home that your family is seeing.

Suggested Action

Embrace the process because sometimes it is uncomfortable and you want to escape. Personal cleansing is a relieving process that takes you into greater freedom, redemption and relief on the other side. Understand that this is a natural process and be willing to let go of the stuff. Let the process flush your mind and emotions, and move on.

This dream can be a call to spend a prolonged period refreshing yourself with foundational truths, get clean and move on with your life. The suggested actions for naked in public dreams also apply here. If specific details are shown to you, pay attention and address any issues that are being revealed.

The bathroom is a natural part of everyday life, so unless there is something revealed in the dream that requires a more demonstrative, proactive response, do your business and move on with your life.

Losing Your Purse or Wallet

Meaning

This dream is a warning to make sure that you are protecting what you have been given. These dreams usually are not literal. Their meaning has to do with your ideas, who you are, what you carry, and what you bring to the table in a business situation and at work. They may also indicate that someone is plotting to rip you off in some way.

Purses and wallets are personal, so this dream is about a personal issue. Your purse or wallet generally carries what identifies you as a unique person, and it represents who you are. Therefore, personal things in your life are being jeopardized: your face (reputation), your finances, your license and the keys to "drive" your vehicle (see also vehicle dreams a few pages ahead). You are losing your identity, or it is being stolen from you.

Questions to Ask

Did someone in the dream steal your purse or wallet, or did you leave it somewhere? What do you carry in there that is very important to you? What other details show you who is involved or what the situation is? If someone stole your item, you are under attack. If you left it somewhere, you are being careless and need to pay attention. Consider what the things inside your purse or wallet might mean metaphorically. Consider also the context of the dream and who is involved, not just the missing purse or wallet.

Suggested Action

Be diligent and pay closer attention. This is a warning to be watchful, take care of what you have been given and make sure it does not get stolen. Step out in who you are. Use your identity and keys to drive the "vehicle" you have been given to accomplish your purpose in life. It is time to fly. (Again, see vehicle dreams a few pages ahead, and see flying dreams, which we already covered.)

Snakes, Reptiles, Alligators

Meaning

Lies and deception are near. This kind of dream may be a tip-off that you are being lied to about something, or that the way you are thinking about something is untruthful. You are being shown that a person or situation is unpredictable, untrustworthy or poisonous and can turn on you at any minute.

The dream can mean that you are believing a lie or that you have been exposed to a lie and it has a hold on you. If the snake bites you, then the lie pertains to a certain aspect of your life. A bite on your hand may symbolize the work of your hands; a bite on your feet may symbolize your path or journey.

Even though some people have these animals as pets, they are not designed to be pets. If you are comfortable around them in your dream, this may represent the fact that you are comfortable with unpredictability or situations where trust is low. For most people, snakes and other reptiles will represent a negative influence of some kind. If you are getting close to a snake, you may be making friends with a lie or with someone who does not have your best interests at heart.

A rare exception would be if an animal like this represents an object of friendship or comfort to the person who had the dream, like a common pet would to most people. The animal then may represent issues of comfort, companionship or whatever the animal has provided for the person.

Questions to Ask

What is the biggest characteristic of the creature? If an alligator is attacking you, its mouth is the biggest feature, which can symbolize gossip that is trying to bite you. If the snake has a long tail or forked tongue, you may encounter a deceptive "tale" that is a mixture of truth and lies.

Other questions to ask are, *Where are the snakes or reptiles in your dream? What is the focus of the attack?* If the animals are around your feet, consider your foundation or what you are walking in right now. If they are snapping at you or jumping out, something may be trying to poison you at a distance or trying to get a jab at you. Use these clues to discern what your dream is trying to tell you.

Suggested Action

Be aware of lies and deception. Consider whether you have been poisoned away from the truth in any way, possibly by vain philosophies through the media or at an institution of higher education. Something you did not know is now being shown to you. Go on a search-and-rescue mission to discover the truth. Remove yourself to a safer place if necessary. Do not swallow everything that comes to you. Process what you receive through a solid value system.

Whatever information you are taking in, secure the integrity of what you are basing your life on in business, finances and with family. What you are being shown can be deadly if it goes unchecked, so deal with the issue wisely.

In life, a buffet table is set before you that contains all kinds of ideas and suggestions. The good is always mixed with the bad, so you must choose wisely which thoughts you will consume and believe as you journey through life. What you feed on, you become. The saying "you are what you eat" is evident here.

Vehicles

Meaning

If you are in a vehicle that you currently own, the dream is about your present life, job or purpose in life. If someone else is driving your vehicle, they have control over something they have not been given. If you are letting them drive and you are along for the ride, then you are giving them control over something that is your responsibility. If you are driving a vehicle that is not yours, you may be stepping outside a boundary by taking control over some thing or situation that is not yours to "drive," so to speak.

Different vehicles will have different meanings. If the vehicle is an airplane, the meaning will be similar to the flying dreams we discussed, in which you are able to move quickly and look at things from a higher altitude. If you are in a train, you are on the right *track* or are in *train*ing. If you are in a fire truck, you may be "putting out a fire" by calming down an argument or getting something under control that is out of control. If you are in a school bus and you are not in school, you are being trained by life. If you are in a ship, it may represent a means to have an international or global impact.

Question to Ask

Vehicle dreams require you to ask a number of questions to get at their meaning. *What is the function of the vehicle, and what is the vehicle doing? Is it the vehicle you currently have? Why are you in a car and not in a plane? Why on a horse and not a donkey?* Compare and contrast. A helicopter is agile and can do things airplanes cannot do. There is a big difference between a passenger plane and a small one-engine plane with just you and someone else inside.

Also ask, *How is the type of vehicle relevant to your life situation right now? Are you observing or participating in the dream?* Usually, the vehicle itself is not the main focus of the dream, but it will provide direction to help interpret the dream accurately. Focus on who is driving. Depending on whether you are an observer or a participant, you are being shown what action is required on your part—how it involves you.

Also consider asking, *Who is on board and where are you going?*

Suggested Action

Remember that the vehicle itself usually is *not* the main focus of the dream. The dream segment that started this chapter, where the little girl was on the large motorcycle, demonstrates this. It was responsibilities too big for her that were making the girl "crash," not an actual motorcycle.

In a vehicle dream, the vehicle tells you what is taking you from place to place, who is with you on the journey and where you are going. Based on this information, take action to ensure you get to the right place at the right time, in the right way and with the right people.

Running in Slow Motion

Meaning

This dream can be so frustrating. You are running and running as hard as you can, and you feel as though your feet are concrete blocks or are stuck in tar. This dream usually means that you are exerting a lot of self-effort, but you are unable to accomplish a task in your own strength. Your strength is failing and you will have to rely on someone or something more powerful than you are to get you where you need to go. You may feel that you are never able to get ahead, even though you are doing everything you know how to do.

Fear may be crippling your efforts to move forward. You are unable to conquer the situation on your own, and you need to get help.

Questions to Ask

When did you have the dream? How many times have you had this dream? The timing of the dream is relevant to whatever situation you were in during the time frame represented. These types of dreams are usually recurring. The number of times you have them can represent how hard you have tried to gain ground in a situation or the amount of hope you have for breakthrough.

Suggested Action

The purpose of this running in slow motion dream is to encourage you to take action, overcome your fears and realize what you have been given. Understand your purpose and start living the life you are supposed to have. Realize that you probably need to get some help and seek out strong support for the specific situation represented. Since perfect love drives out fear, get "love" involved in this situation—love from others you can trust and from God. (See 1 John 4:18 in the Bible.)

This type of dream usually comes at a time when something is changing in your life and you have reached the end of your rope. Your inability to accomplish this task in and of yourself is playing out in your dream. Involve God and He will direct your path, taking the frustration away and giving you guidance and power for your forward motion.

Unable to Speak or Scream

Meaning

This type of dream has to do with your voice. You are losing your voice, or you are not being heard. If you are scared and you cannot scream, fear is crippling you. Fear is taking away the confidence to use your voice for something you believe in.

If you are trying to scream and nothing comes out, fear is causing you to do nothing instead of reaching out for help. If you are unable to speak in your dream, the people you are speaking to may not be in a place where they can hear you, or you have a message but the door to share has not yet been opened.

This dream is showing you that you are dealing with a negative force that is trying to keep you quiet, or that something is trying to paralyze your voice, contrary to who you were designed to be. This dream can be showing your response to this darkness, which is often fear of some kind. It can also be awakening you to break negative thoughts about your self-worth and understand the value of what you have to say.

Questions to Ask

What is scaring you or keeping you down? Is it others' opinions of you? Your own insecurity? Messages you have been told since you were young? How long has this been happening? Be aware that whatever is setting itself against your voice or against you speaking out is trying to steal your future.

Also ask, *Who are you speaking to in the dream, and how does it relate to your life right now? What might be trying to keep you from speaking out?*

Suggested Action

If something is chasing you, follow the suggested actions in the being chased dream section we already covered. Turn and face it, and do not let it control you. These unable to speak or scream dreams are a call to be bold and decisive. Act now and use your voice courageously, because you are made to overcome.

Understand that the goal of this darkness coming against you is to isolate you and keep you from reaching out for help. Reach out to God and others for help. Your ability to humble yourself and submit to an authority structure that has a higher power of ultimate good will give you the power you need to deal with any bad thing attacking you. If you are encountering darkness, you need to position yourself in a light that is bigger than you are.

This dream is also a call to use discernment in *how* and *when* to use your voice. Use the voice you have been given for a good cause. Determine the ability of your audience to hear and respond to your message. Similar to the suggested actions in the flying or swimming dream section, be bold and use your voice to share your unique perspective and insight. Your voice is supposed to be a force for good to bring freedom to others.

Earthquakes or Tidal Waves

Meaning

This type of dream can be literal or metaphorical. Something is getting ready to be shaken, and things will not stay as they are now. Your foundations are being shaken or removed to get you to a better place. The effects of an earthquake are widespread. In your dream, if you experience an earthquake at work, a big change may be coming—possibly a change of leadership. Something may be shaken that will affect everyone in the office. If the earthquake is at home, then a shaking is coming to your family. People will wake up, and things will get sorted out.

If you experience a tidal wave in your dream, you may be involved in something over your head. Either that, or you are being taken away and deposited somewhere else by a powerful force.

Often, earthquake or tidal wave dreams are positive and show that a change is coming that will have a big impact on who you are, what you are doing and where you are going.

If the shaking in your dream happens in another location geographically, you could be seeing a disaster that may literally happen in another place. If you have a track record of having dreams that foretell future events, tell others so that some kind of precautions can be taken.

Questions to Ask

Where does the earthquake or tidal wave take place? Who was involved in the event? Consider your connection to the area involved, and think about whether the people involved were your family, others you know or people you do not recognize at all.

Ask also, *Have you had the dream more than once?* If it occurs more than once, pay attention because you are being shown the significance of what is coming. Also be aware that dreams foretelling literal events usually come more than once.

Suggested Action

Get ready. Be expecting something. Understand that things will not be as they were. See the event as an opportunity, not a catastrophe (assuming it is not a literal event). Something old is being removed, and something new is taking its place. Do what you can to prepare so that you can survive the shaking or ride the wave, and help others as much as you can.

If you feel it is a literal dream, alert others you know and find out if they are having similar dreams. Understand that you are being given this dream because you can get the word out to help prevent unnecessary loss.

Taking a Test / Going Back to School

Meaning

You are missing something you need in order to pass a test. You are unprepared, or you feel ill-equipped for a challenge. The way you are doing something may be off the mark, which is causing you to take the test again—until you pass it. The dream could be pointing to a character issue or a skill set you need to succeed at work or home.

These dreams often reoccur to help you realize that you need to make corrections in order to "graduate" or move on in life. Pay attention to details around the context of such a dream. For example, if you do not have something to write with in the dream, it may be a picture showing you that you need to take action of some kind to be prepared for whatever is ahead.

Similar to a vehicle dream where you are on a bus, there may be a life lesson that you are supposed to learn if you have a school or test dream. It can be a metaphor for where you are in your growth as a person.

If you are in middle school in your dream, you are beyond the primary lesson, but there are things you need to learn before you get to *high* school, with higher learning. This will prepare you for your life's work. These dreams can happen throughout life and apply to different areas of your life in which you still need to learn and grow.

Questions to Ask

How many times have you had the dream? What test are you taking? What school are you at? What class do you have to take? Identify the kind of test and why you must to take it more than once. Identify the place and the subject.

Suggested Action

Pay attention to the area of your life the dream is highlighting. Be a student of what is happening around you. Gain more understanding about what you need to do to pass the test or why you are going back to school. Be teachable. Learn the lesson and make the needed adjustments so you can move on with your purpose in life. School is synonymous with teaching, so be teachable and learn from those around you and from life's circumstances.

Common Elements with Customized Solutions

I have found that the dream themes we have covered in this chapter, as well as some other dream themes, are common around the world. The dream symbol appendix at the back of this book covers many common elements found in people's dreams.

Remember, however, that most of your dreams are directed toward *your* needs and pursuits. They are meant to provide you with customized solutions for the situations you face in life.

TAKEAWAYS

- You have your own dream language. Start to learn it.
- Your dreams are meant to help you be the best you can be and make the most of your life.
- Have you had a dream with one of these themes? What do you think this dream is telling you based on what you read in this chapter?

5

TYPES OF DREAMS AND THEIR INTERPRETATIONS

Situation: Hidden secret.

Dream: I had a dream in which I was asking my husband if he was stealing from us. He told me in the dream that he was not, but I knew he was lying to me. I woke up crying, and I told my husband the dream. He laughed at me and said he would never do something like that.

Solution: Two months later, he admitted to hiding money from me so that he could buy something he wanted. He also said, "I can never get away with anything when I'm around you." This dream helped me see a problem I did not know existed.

While dreams come in many types, in this chapter I will focus on four main types that I encounter when I talk to people, along with their interpretations. They are what I call warning dreams, direction dreams, self-revealing dreams and spiritual realm dreams.

Warning Dreams

Warning dreams often contain imagery such as snakes or spiders. The snakes can symbolize deception or represent low, slithering, sometimes poisonous messages or "tales." The spiders can represent biting or stinging hindrances to your future. Warning dreams can also contain tornados, which can characterize your life as somehow spinning out of control, and tidal waves or flooding, which can show that you are in over your head on some issues. Warning dreams are like a spiritual thermometer that will give you a heads-up as you proceed through life.

Warning dreams seem to carry more of a punch than other types of dreams. They are often extremely real, vivid and visual. After a person has a warning dream, that dream is "branded" on his or her soul and is impossible to forget.

In my travels, I have met people who have dreamed of actual events before they happened, like 9/11, earthquakes, tidal waves, fires, tornados and other disasters. If you will pay attention to the dreams you are receiving, you may be able to avoid being in the wrong place at the wrong time. Not all dreams with this kind of imagery are literal dreams, but they can be if the dreamer has an active dream life where dreams are literal and really do come to pass.

Let's look at some examples of warning dreams, along with their interpretations.

Don't Swallow Everything You Are Told

I once ran into a university student who shared that he dreamed his professor was shoving a snake down his throat sideways and that he was choking on it. He happened to be studying psychology at the time and was having a hard time swallowing all that he was being taught. The snake in this dream represented a big lie that this person was being force-fed, and it seemed as though his internal "truth detector" was not allowing him to receive the information.

Often our spirits inside us will send a signal to our minds that something is not right. When we get this "nudge," we must purpose to pay attention to the warning and search out the truth. Simply adhering to this signal can help us avoid pitfalls and false paths we might be considering. The university student's dream was showing him that the truth he had on the inside was not allowing him to process the lie he was being taught, so his system was kicking it out.

Your Lifestyle May Lead to Death

A man in San Antonio, Texas, told someone on our team about a dream where he saw himself run out the front door of his house and cross his front yard. As he was running, a shot fired from a passing car hit him, and he fell to the ground and died. This was clearly a warning dream.

The image of a front door can show a person entering into future events, and a back door can represent going into the past. Our impression of this man was that he had involved himself in some dangerous activities, and his life choices were putting him in danger of an early death. Our interpreter told him that God was warning him in this dream, and that if he did not make a lifestyle change immediately, he would be in danger of losing his life. We are not sure what the man did with the information, but he was given the message. Hopefully he received it and followed the advice.

A Tsunami Is Coming

Another example of a warning dream comes from a man in the southern part of India. He lived on the island just above Sri Lanka, and his dream told him of a flood where houses, people, animals and everything else in his village was washed away by this violent wave of water. He awoke and alerted his friends in not only his village, but also in the surrounding villages. Those who heard the dream heeded it. They gathered together and prayed. When the tsunami hit, the water miraculously split and went around the village, sparing not only the people of the village, but also all of their livestock. Not even a chicken was lost. This is an example of a literal warning dream. Thankfully, the man responded appropriately and saved many people in the process.

I often wonder how many people have dreams about global disasters before they happen. After the tsunami that hit Japan in March 2011, I received an email from a woman who had documented a dream about this event. She had the dream the first week of January 2010. Upon waking from it, she called her sister and told her that Japan would be struck by a tsunami. Here are key parts of her dream from her journal:

> I had a dream that I was inside an airport along the coast of Japan. As I proceeded forward through the body of the airport, I heard a noise, and when I turned around, I saw the entire place engulfed with water. People were floating and swirling up to the ceiling. When I realized what was taking place, a force pulled me through a set of glass doors to the side of a room. I could see the people drowning through the door that was now closed. This room was dry, and no water leaked through. As this force pulled me through the middle of the room, it pulled my sister and niece to my side. Toward the other end of this room was the beginning swirl of "the yellow brick road." Each of us placed a foot on it and began to walk forward toward another set of glass doors, which were opened and led outside to high and dry ground with the sun shining.

Playing with Deception

Warning dreams have been given to parents regarding their children. I know of one couple who had young daughters, and the husband had a dream about a snake that had wrapped itself around a light in their house. The daughters were on a ladder, trying to awaken the snake so they could play with it. They were intrigued by the snake and wanted to see what its reaction would be if they poked at it. The husband climbed the ladder and saw the snake. The snake awoke and started chasing him. He took the snake and wrung its neck so that it could not harm his daughters.

In the dream, the girls were being attracted to this snake in the light that was on the *ceiling*, which was showing that it represented a high-level lie. Because it was in a light fixture, the meaning had to do with a false light—something that was illuminated but was providing false direction. This dream alerted the couple to address some adolescent mischief in their daughters. The girls were playing with something deceptively dangerous. As their parents, this couple started paying more attention to the girls' activities so they could take steps to protect their children.

Responding to Warning Dreams

What is a good response to a warning dream? Listen to the message, determine wisely what the dream may be telling you and then do something about it. If you dream something and it really does happen the way you dreamed it, it is vitally important that you pay attention to future warning dreams. If you feel your dream could be warning you about something, then take the time to investigate.

If your dream contains information about your work, then what was the dream telling you? Search out the meaning first before making any decision to take action on what the dream is saying. Hasty actions regarding information or direction in dreams may only cause a situation to get worse before it gets better, especially if you are dreaming about a certain person or an actual event.

Warning dreams are not given to incite fear or cause panic, but they could be looked at as a "yellow flashing light" to give you a sign to move with caution. Timing is usually involved. Some dreams require that you take action right away. In other situations, the dream will let you know that something is coming but is not yet here.

Remember that if you choose to involve yourself in situations that are dangerous and you have a warning dream, then you are responsible to adjust your behavior to prevent an early departure from this earth.

Direction Dreams

Direction dreams help you make timely, necessary changes so you can head down the right path into your destiny. If you dream that you cannot pass a test, forget the numbers to a locker, cannot find your way out of a building, are having trouble getting in the game or are running in slow motion, you may be having a direction dream.

These direction dreams can seem frustrating at times, but they are necessary because they alert and awaken you to a different way of engaging with your future. Let's look at a few examples of direction dreams, along with their interpretations.

Get into the Game

At the Sundance Film Festival, I encountered a man who had experienced the same dream four nights a week for seven years. When you think about it, having a recurring dream that many times must be tormenting! In his dream, he was always trying to get into a baseball game. Each time, in one way or another he was faced with obstacles that prevented him from obtaining this goal. In one dream, he could not find his baseball mitt or bat. In another dream, he was late and missed the game. In another, he could not get his locker open. The dream scenario was the same, but with different hindrances.

As I listened to his dreams, it became clear that the pathway he was currently on was not opening up a way for him to fulfill his destiny. He had a vision of where he wanted to be in life, but it seemed that everything was against him. I suggested that he reconsider how he was going about obtaining his goal.

As the dream interpretation unfolded, the dreamer suddenly gained insight into what had been preventing him from "getting into the game" of life. When he realized what was holding him back, he was ecstatic and began running around the room, jumping and shouting. Mystery solved! Unlocking the dream and gaining some understanding gave him not only relief from a perplexing and disturbing dream, but direction about how to get on the path of success.

Keep Going Even in a Fog

A woman told me about a clear direction dream she had in which she was in her car, traveling up a mountain with her eleven-year-old daughter. As she ascended the hill, suddenly a fog settled in and she could not see the road. She stopped the car because of the lack of visibility. Men dressed in hoods approached the car from behind and were trying to get in. The woman frantically tried to lock the doors, while her daughter screamed at her to start the car and keep going.

The interpretation was that this woman was headed to another level in life, and her decision to move forward was also affecting her daughter. The message was to keep going, even if she did not clearly see what was in front of her. Her choice to stop caused her to be tormented by things from her past, which could keep her and her daughter from obtaining their goals in life if she did not get moving again.

Once again, the dreamer was excited about understanding the meaning of this dream, and she knew exactly what to do in response. She had to keep going and move steadily forward until the "fog" cleared and the light revealed more of the path ahead. This is true in our lives. Just because we do not have all the details about our journey, that does not mean we stagnate or refuse to move forward. "Fogged" vision is temporary and lifts as we continue on our way.

You Will Ascend to Your Creative Destiny

Other direction dreams can involve hallways. Hallways in the natural move us from one room to another. Hallways can also provide multiple opportunities for us, depending on which door we choose to go through.

A young man transitioning in his film/music career told me of a dream he had about falling off a trapeze into a filthy bathroom where a lion was behind a sliding door. He went down a hallway and joined Michael Jackson, who was going up an escalator. Michael Jackson then turned into a very large woman.

This seemed like a complicated dream, but when I broke it down, I understood that these images pertained to this young man's destiny. The trapeze represented something he was unskilled at. Falling into the bathroom signified that he would go through a place of cleansing, where a lion—a protector—would try to get into his life. The protector—someone more powerful than himself—would meet him in a place of weakness where spiritual cleansing would take place. He then went down a hallway and transitioned up an escalator with Michael Jackson, who turned into a very large woman. She was like one of those giant balloon characters that handlers walk along a parade route, and she was taking up lots of room and getting lots of attention.

Those images signified that on his journey into his destiny, this young man would be guided into ascending to his place of colorful creativity, visibility and usefulness. The implications of his dream—and consequently the plans for his life—were much bigger than he originally thought.

How to Fix a Machine

Floyd Ragsdale was an employee at DuPont, a science-based products and services company founded in 1802. He was having trouble with a machine that manufactured Kevlar fiber, the material in bulletproof vests. The machine's downtime cost the company $700 a minute, so everyone was working diligently to solve the problem. Nothing was solving it, however, until Ragsdale had a dream:

> One night, Ragsdale, an engineer with no college education, had a dream in which he saw the tubes of a machine and springs. He came to work the next day and told his boss about the dream. He received a typical reaction: his boss scoffed and told him to forget about it. When Ragsdale's shift ended, he went ahead and inserted springs into the tubes, and the machine worked perfectly, saving the company more than $3 million! [1]

Ragsdale had many other dreams that provided direction about how to address workplace problems that others were unable to solve.

Responding to Direction Dreams

When you have a direction dream, see it as an opportunity to make a positive and significant change that will head you more directly on a path toward greater success. I like to think of direction dreams as heads-up messages telling us to examine our current life path.

Direction dreams can also bring to the surface repressed feelings of "never measuring up" or "always falling short." Be careful that they do not put you into failure mode or keep you there. If they discourage you, they could cause you to neglect taking the actions necessary to overcome your obstacles and accomplish your goals. If pulling back in discouragement is your first inclination after having a direction dream, the dream could be coming from a Lie source (we will talk more about the sources of dreams in the next chapter).

The fact is that we can succeed at whatever we set our minds and hearts to do. Repetitive patterns of failure do not have to continue dictating our future. If that kind of pattern has been the case for you, take a direction dream as an opportunity to make positive changes now in your mind, heart and life. Always, always, always think the best first and plan to succeed.

Self-Revealing Dreams

As their name suggests, self-revealing dreams are dreams that reveal what is really going on inside a person. These dreams come to us at night as a result of our daytime activity. Self-revealing dreams tell us what our lives are really like. Sometimes they reveal our irrational fears, and many times they cause anxiety.

Dreams like these go something like, "I dreamed my boyfriend was cheating on me with my best friend." Now, if that were truly the case, then you would have a problem. But if, in fact, he is *not* cheating on you, then this dream may be revealing rejection issues you have on the inside, along with a fear of abandonment. Most often, what you are fearful about during your waking hours can play out in various scenarios in your dreams.

Self-revealing dreams can cause you to doubt yourself, doubt those around you and scrutinize everything in your world. Or they can just be crazy and often humorous dreams with nothing much in them making sense, yet you still remember them. Let's look at a few examples of self-revealing dreams, along with their interpretations.

No More Performance

In this dream, a woman was driving down the street where she grew up, and a policeman pulled her car over. The officer asked her if she had a mop in the car. Oddly enough, she did. The officer asked her to get out of the car and show him how the mop worked. She noticed the mop was worn and in bad shape, but she began to mop the street using all of her force. From the corner of her eye, she noticed that another car had been stopped for the same reason. The officer told her not to go anywhere until morning. She also

73

noticed there were speed bumps on the road, which was interesting because her childhood street did not have speed bumps.

How would you interpret this dream? Remember that it is important to look through the framework I shared in chapter 3. The purpose of this dream was for this woman's good—to bring her into a greater place of freedom and joy in life.

As I listened to this dream, the meaning began to unfold. Ever since she was a little girl, this woman had been rewarded if she worked hard. The officer, being an authority figure, was identifying this trap in her life as he asked her to demonstrate mopping with a worn-out mop. The fact that the mop was worn also told me she had been in this "performance" mode for a long time. The speed bumps were an indication that she ought to slow down and regain her value and self-worth, apart from working or performing for them. From the part she related where the officer told her not to go anywhere until morning, I understood that a new day was coming where she would be free to live her life, regain her childhood and play again.

The woman felt this dream accurately depicted her life. Encouragement and freedom rose up in her heart as she embraced this interpretation and made new choices to abandon a false value system.

A Controlling Boyfriend

A woman in a relationship once told me a dream that involved her boyfriend. In her dream, he was driving her car and she was in the passenger seat. As she looked to the right (away from her boyfriend), his face appeared and started talking and laughing with her. She was enjoying the experience with the talking face, but then she looked back to the left at her boyfriend driving the car, and her heart dropped into sadness.

The interpretation of this woman's dream was that her boyfriend had taken a dominant place in her life (he was driving *her* car).

When the boyfriend's face appeared to her right, this represented the way things used to be between them, before he began asserting himself in the relationship and taking over. When she looked back to her boyfriend driving her car, her heart was sad because the relationship had started out as so much fun and so exciting, but now it was something else. She found through the dream that she was longing to return again to her earlier and better relationship with this man.

Son Dies from a Head Wound

A tarot card reader approached me to tell me about a horrifying dream she had that involved her son. In this dream, her eight-year-old son was in a coffin. The cause of death was a head injury. She had dreamed this dream three times in a week, so now she was fearful that it was a literal warning dream.

When I heard her dream, I prayed and asked God if it was a true warning dream. The answer I received was, "What did the child die from?" I thought, *from a head wound.* I then saw that the dream had something to do with his mind and his thinking. The interpretation was simple when I understood that the child was not going to die a natural death. This eight-year-old boy was growing in his ability to understand many things, especially spiritual things. The head wound indicated that he would have a different understanding on these matters than his mother, and she would have to deal with the fact that he most likely would not follow in her spiritual path. I encouraged her to let him pursue his own spiritual journey and let the Spirit of Truth be his guide. I told her that her son had a gift from God and that his mind most likely would not work the way hers does.

I saw this woman a year later. Her son, by then nine, was healthy and was advancing in understanding his prophetic gift. He was even reading the Bible and other books of spiritual significance. I was very glad my interpretation proved correct! A literal interpretation of her dream about his death would have been a hard message to deliver to a mother about her child.

Faces Peeling Off

A young man related this dream to me:

> My girlfriend and I were at a party, and we were getting ready to have sex. All of a sudden, I noticed her face was peeling off as she was scratching her face. We both started screaming, and I noticed that my face was peeling off also.

This dream was showing that these two people were in transition. Faces represent image and identity. With both of their faces peeling off, the dream was indicating that another expression was being revealed, kind of like a mask coming off. This dream showed me that their relationship was changing. Most likely, it was moving into more of a deep commitment rather than just being a fling.

Responding to Self-Revealing Dreams

You can see by these examples that self-revealing dreams, if discerned and acted upon wisely, can be encouraging and powerful. They can bring you into a greater place of freedom in who you are supposed to be. When you have a dream that reveals something about yourself, it is like looking into a mirror. Some things you can change; other things are just part of who you are. Either way, such dreams can be an encouragement for the dreamer to keep growing and changing for the better.

Interpreting a self-revealing dream properly can prevent you from making a compulsive choice to act on a dream's message. (Remember, not all messages are what they seem.) In other words, do not chase a certain guy or girl because you had a dream that the two of you got married. The dream could come because you want something so badly, not because it is a true dream that you should follow. With the more serious choices in life such as getting married, moving, taking a new job or other larger life decisions, many more confirmations will come your way. Those kinds of decisions should be based on more than just a single dream.

Spiritual Realm Dreams

In one sense, all dreams are spiritual because we are spiritual beings. And all dreams give you insight into what is not clearly seen. For the purpose of putting dreams into a few main categories, though, I am defining spiritual realm dreams as those that have a notable spiritual message and provide a preview into the spiritual realm. They often contain images such as angels or demons, heaven or hell, the afterlife and things of a spiritual nature.

Our physical senses can deceive us, blocking us from perceiving spiritual truths. Spiritual realm dreams give insight into this realm that we often do not perceive with our senses. They come to us so that we can take action and bring spiritual realities into the natural world.

Judgment Day

At the Sundance Film Festival, a young man approached me with a bunch of his friends. He shared a recent dream that had come his way while he was spending the night at a friend's house. In the dream, he saw himself get out of bed and get into his car. He began driving home down the freeway and had a wreck that took his life. He could see the crumpled car and people standing around looking at his car with him inside it. Some people were crying as they saw this horrible accident. He then looked around and saw that he was before Jesus Christ on Judgment Day. He said there were two lines of people. One line was going to heaven, and one line was going to hell. He said he was in the middle of the two lines.

After telling us this dream, he asked us if he was going to die. I paused for a moment to get his attention and then told him, "Yes, we're all going to die, but the good news is that you have a chance to figure out which line you want to be in before you die."

"But I don't really believe in God," he said.

I moved closer to him and said, "Dude, it was your dream, not mine."

My message to him was that he had to deal with the reality of the message he had been given. This spiritual realm dream was a warning to be wise about what path he would choose in life. Just because his belief system did not support his dream did not mean that his dream should not be taken seriously.

This young man tried to be cool around his friends by seeking to get out of the interpretation since it dealt with having to take responsibility for his life choices and belief systems. I did not try to persuade him or preach to him; I simply revealed the message given in the dream. (And this dream was actually pretty easy to interpret.) Ultimately, his heart would know the importance of the dream, even if his mind did not agree.

Demon Trying to Kill a Person

One person related this spiritual realm dream to me:

I have had dreams of physical demonic attacks that should have been fatal, except I would not die. For example, a few nights ago, a demon was trying to kill me, and it dug its nails into my side to rip out my organs. It did hurt, but then the pain lessened and turned into an annoying stinging. Then I flew away in one piece, but the demon held on.

This person has a life to live and is not going to be taken out early. The fact that the demon dug its nails into the side of the dreamer to get at the organs tells me that it was most likely after the dreamer's heart. But in this dream, the dreamer was able to fly away in one piece, even though the demon held on.

This dreamer needs a power stronger and more protective to take charge of his or her life. Flying in the dream told me that the dreamer has the ability to live above attacks and is not limited to the natural realm alone.

Responding to Spiritual Realm Dreams

Spiritual realm dreams give a person an opportunity to respond to a greater truth than the one he or she is presently experiencing. You cannot argue with a dream, especially when it is captivating and plays out like a movie. Let's face it—there are things we just are unaware of, and when we are faced with clear spiritual activity in a dream, we cannot dismiss it. As humans we have a spirit, so spiritual realm dreams are very real and speak clearly to that part of us.

If you are visited by an angel or a demon in your dreams, you have to look at the timing. Ask yourself, *Why is this happening now? What is the message?* Then determine the action to take in response.

If the dream is from a heavenly realm, then it is usually so vivid that it can rock your world. If an angel is in the dream, usually there is a message of importance you need to pay close attention to. If a demon is in the dream, it could most likely show up to hinder you or to bring fear into a situation you are dealing with.

The Western world has turned the spiritual realm into make-believe, but the spiritual realm is very real—we should pay attention to it.

Continue the Search

While there are other types of dreams, these four types of dreams—warning dreams, direction dreams, self-revealing dreams and spiritual realm dreams—are the ones that I tend to interpret the most. The purpose of the information in this chapter is to help you better interpret your dreams and know what to do with their messages.

Mystery often surrounds a high-impact dream. Dreams are also layered. The first layer is the initial interpretation based on the context of the dream. Over time, however, new layers are revealed as more understanding unlocks other angles or viewpoints of the dream. Each layer gives the dreamer deeper insight into the message the dream reveals.

Continue to search out the meaning of the dreams you receive. Apply the principles we have covered so far; they will help you look deeper than the first thing you see. So will the pages ahead. Next, let's look at three main steps to take in dream interpretation and how you can apply this information to your dreams.

TAKEAWAYS

- You are dreaming for a reason. Search out the meaning of your dreams.

- Warning dreams, direction dreams, self-revealing dreams and spiritual realm dreams can provide important information you need to succeed in life.

- What are your types of dreams telling you?

6

HOW TO INTERPRET
YOUR DREAMS

Situation: I desperately needed a good car but did not have the time or patience to go out and look for one.

Dream: I dreamed that my dad took me to a car dealership and asked me what kind of car I wanted. Although my dad had passed away years previously, in the dream he represented how I was loved and how I would be provided for—receiving just what I needed, the same as I had experienced when he was alive.

Solution: This dream encouraged me to start looking for a car. (I had been really discouraged because of my lack of good transportation.) About a month later, I found a car with little effort that was just perfect for me.

In its simplest form, dream interpretation involves asking yourself a couple of questions: *What am I supposed to receive from this dream? Why did I have this dream now?* I want to look at three steps you can take to help you answer those questions. These three steps are:

- Determine the source
- Determine the message
- Determine your action

It is extremely important to know how to interpret your dreams properly so that you do not miss out on what is being given to you as you sleep. While some dreams are simply a manifestation of what went on during the day, other dreams can inspire the pursuit of impossibilities—or what you once thought impossible before the dream. The way you interpret what you are given is just as important as a dream itself. Being guided by the wrong interpretation of a dream that is supposed to provide direction is like following a GPS that gives you the wrong directions to your destination.

I was listening to a syndicated radio program where people would call in and tell their dreams to a guy who would give an interpretation. Unfortunately, the dream interpreter would give a mind-processed interpretation that was methodical and unrelated to the essence of the dream, which would totally misguide the interpretation so that the dreamers were no better off after telling him their dreams than they were before.

On this radio show, a woman called in who dreamed she had been invited to a church service with her friend. This woman had never attended church before, but she knew that the preacher was getting ready to give a message that she needed to hear to help her in life. She said that in her dream, she was on the edge of her seat as she listened to the preacher.

Suddenly, someone took her by the hand and led her out, enticing her into a side room where someone was waiting to read her palm. She wanted to get back to the service where the preacher was speaking because she knew he had a message for her, but the door was stuck and she could not get out.

The dream interpreter told her that her consciousness knew the true message she needed to hear, and that was why she was led into the side room to get her palm read. He told her to listen to her own thoughts, which she had just admitted had gotten her into situations that had not been good for her. The end result of his interpretation was that a clear, God-given dream was twisted around by psychobabble, and she was sent on a journey down a side road that was not where she was supposed to be and would lead nowhere.

What this woman should have been told is that there was a message she needed to hear, and there were sources trying to keep her from hearing it. These distracting sources were giving her a different message than her dream and were pulling her away from the truth into a place of isolation.

The purpose of dreams is to give you hope and power to live the right life for you. They provide encouragement and guidance on your life path to a better place. If you are willing to go, your dreams will send you on a search—a journey to discover the truth. Sometimes you gain as much through the searching process as you do from the final message of a dream.

While I think you should pay attention to all of your dreams, I highly recommend paying the closest attention to these:

- The same dream occurring more than once
- Different dreams that have a similar theme
- Dreams that are so vivid, you feel as if you were there

Stop for a moment and think of a dream you have had that falls into one of these three categories. Can you think of one? Now take a few minutes and turn to the dream journal at the back of this book. Use the format provided to write down your dream. Also keep that dream in mind as we look at the three steps to dream interpretation I just mentioned: determine the source, determine the message and determine your action.

Step 1: Determine the Source

The question I most often hear is, "Are all dreams from God?" The answer is no. There are three sources of dreams, which I call Self, Lie and Truth. A dream can come from just one of these sources, or since dreams are layered, where a dream comes from can be layered, too. You can have a Self dream that has Truth or Lie mixed in. (I will talk more about that in the pages ahead.)

Learning your own dream language and discerning the right interpretation for your dreams is a journey. Go for it and enjoy it! Knowing about these three sources of dreams will come in handy. Let's look at the nature of each source I have mentioned.

Dreams from Self

Ancient wisdom literature has said, "For a dream comes through much activity, and a fool's voice is known by his many words" (Ecclesiastes 5:3). Your daily activities will come out in your dream life. For example, one night before going to bed I was playing a video game where I had to find a hidden object. That night I had a dream that I was hunting for stuff. You might go to a store and have an encounter with a salesperson and dream about that person that night. A dream like this has nothing to do with anything except that you are "flushing" your system to get rid of what you encountered during the day.

Other dreams reveal something that goes beyond the things that affected you during the day. I have talked to people who have dreamed that a spouse or significant other is cheating on them. What is often going on is that such people carry so much suspicion and past hurt that they dream about betrayal shattering something important to them.

You may dream that a co-worker you do not like is doing something against you. Dreams can reveal suspicion in places where you do not have much trust. They also can expose the real image you have of yourself and others. If you do not interpret these Self dreams properly, they can foster a mindset that will cause you to undermine your potential for success. Even if something is going well for you, you could destroy it because you do not know any other way to proceed—you are too used to things getting blown up.

Self dreams often have to do with what is going on in your thoughts and emotions at the time of the dream, or with things that you want to happen in the future. You dream that something happens because you want it so badly, but it is not necessarily supposed to happen. You have self-will, and that language will express itself in your dreams.

Be careful, however, not to discount a dream because you think it is a Self dream. It could be a Truth dream, which we will talk about just ahead. Usually, a Truth dream will happen more than once, or you will have a number of dreams around the same theme.

A dream from Self is not necessarily bad, nor should it be discounted. It is showing you something about yourself. For example, a dream about being naked in public may reveal how exposed you are feeling in a vulnerable situation. While this Self dream is just showing you what is going on inside yourself, you could take it as an opportunity either to be okay with yourself or to make some positive corrections in your behavior.

Dreams from Lie

A dream from Lie will come to sabotage your success and keep you from doing what you are meant to do. Lying dreams can influence you to do something that in the end will not benefit you. They may tell you that you are supposed to marry this person or buy that stock or quit your job, and what they are telling you may look really close to the truth, but it may not be the right thing to do. It is important that you discern the meaning of all of your dreams carefully and not jump to a quick conclusion. Taking action without taking some time to search out the true meaning of a dream will not benefit you.

Lying dreams also come to accuse others. I see this all the time in my dream schools. Someone will share a dream and immediately use its negative images to reveal something bad about a person, an organization or whatever—all because the dreamer has an unresolved issue with the perceived focus of his or her dream. To come to these negative conclusions in this way and act on them is both dangerous and destructive.

You may have a dream about someone—maybe someone you have a good opinion of—but you dream they are doing something bad like stealing from you or doing drugs. The purpose of this Lie dream is to stir you up and bring about discord so that you are suspicious, where you never would have entertained suspicions before the dream.

It is one thing if a dream shows you something that you need to pay attention to, but such a message would come to you in other ways besides a dream. A spiritual enemy does exist whose goal is to steal, kill and destroy. If you have a dream with the themes of stealing, killing or destroying (literally or figuratively), then understand that something may be trying to get in your way and hinder your destiny. And if this enemy can kill a relationship through lying dreams, or bring accusation against someone who is supposed to be a close friend, he wins and you lose. The end result of lying dreams is distrust that keeps that relationship in a prison. Love always thinks the best of other people first.

Lying dreams also tell you wrong things about yourself—like you are fat or you are stupid. They keep you from being released into your purpose in life.

As I said earlier, the source of a dream can be layered. For example, let's say you are focused on winning the lottery, and you are buying tickets to position yourself to win so that you can be rich. Because of your actions, you could have a Self dream one night that you win the lottery. You act on that dream and buy even more tickets. Then a Lie dream might come along that reinforces your wish and gets you to act on your desire even more. If the enemy is successful at his lies, he can trick you into acting irresponsibly often enough that your desire disrupts your relationships and pulls you into negative and addictive behaviors.

Dreams from a lying source are often fear-based; they try to scare you or keep you from something. For instance, a person who has been in a bad place and is trying to make positive changes in life may have a dream that leaves him or her with a sense of failure and hopelessness. The dream probably has nothing to do with the person's future or personal life. It will contain enough truth to make it seem real, but the enemy is only trying to instill fear so that this person gives up and stops reaching for a better tomorrow. The person's response should be one of courage to rise up against this enemy and overcome it—or to get around a few other people who can help him or her accomplish the honorable goal of freedom.

A Lie dream can happen when the chips are down or when you have a big decision to make. The purpose is to get you to back down, be fearful or hopeless, anticipate failure or expect the worse. Just like Self dreams, Lie dreams can foster a mindset that will cause you to undermine your potential for success. If the enemy can get you to blow up your own future, then there is less work for him to do.

How to Flip Your Dreams

Before we look at the third source, dreams from Truth, let's take a minute to look at how to "flip" your dreams. No matter what the source of your dreams, with some wisdom and discernment you can flip a dream to understand what is really going on. Consider the following dreams and how you could flip them to work for you and not against you.

- You have a dream that something valuable is taken from you in a forceful manner, which leaves you with feelings of fear and anxiety. It is a good idea to protect yourself and the things that are important to you from intruders. However, if this is a lying dream, the enemy is trying to get you to be overly cautious and shut down emotionally—maybe in a relationship that is actually good for you.

To flip this dream, you need to realize that you have something valuable that is worth taking. Because of this thing's value, an evil force is making an effort to kill it, destroy it or steal it from you so that it does not have the impact it was made for.

- You have a dream that a treasured pet is killed. This pet that has brought you comfort is violently taken away from you by someone you know. If such a dream hits your emotions with no real message other than fear, the dream is from the enemy, who is trying to instill fear of loss in you.

When our daughter was about seven years old, she had a dream that our family was in heaven, but in a waiting area that looked like an old camper. A bunch of our furniture was in the camper, and we had our dog, Patches, with us. God was moving stuff around as if He was really busy, and when He got to us, He said, "There are no dogs allowed in heaven." He then took our dog and broke her paw, and she died.

Our daughter was traumatized by that dream, which was clearly a lying dream sent to paint a horrible picture of God. To flip this dream, we took the opportunity to reinforce to our daughter God's loving, comforting character. She was in a time of spiritual growth in her life and was asking many questions about God. The enemy used this lying image of God torturing our dog because our daughter loved our dog very much. The enemy wanted to use the Lie dream to turn our daughter's heart away from a positive spiritual experience, but we flipped it and talked to her about the goodness of God.

To flip a lying dream like this, you will need to discern *what* the enemy is trying to do and *why*. Then take action to reinforce the truth that counteracts the message of the lying dream. The most important part of flipping a dream from Lie or even from Self is to resist the temptation to become fearful, depressed or hindered in any way. The enemy will do what it takes to trip you up and will use lying dreams in an attempt to cheat you out of a good future.

While I was in Switzerland, a girl came to me in tears. She had made a major shift in her life and was taking huge strides to come out of old, destructive habits and behavior patterns. But every night, she was being tormented by dreaming about the old things she used to do. This Lie dream was accusing her with the message, "You're not becoming a better person—look at what you've done. This is who you really are!"

While she knew the truth, the lying dreams were haunting her even though the bad stuff was no longer part of her life. To flip her dreams, every morning she had to reprogram her thinking and tell herself that what she had dreamed was *not* who she was anymore and that she was *not* going to give in to those negative behaviors.

The lesson to be learned here is to listen to the messages you are hearing around you—whether from your dreams or from friends or some other positive influence—but listen with insight and discernment. No matter what you believe the source is of a dream with a message, ask yourself the question, *Why did I have this dream?* Seek out a meaning, be prepared and take courageous action. Do not be discouraged by the dream or dismiss it.

Dreams from Truth

We have seen how dreams can come from Self and from Lie, and how they can be flipped to help and not hinder you. Dreams can also come from Truth. If you were to say to me, "Tell me the truth," I am guessing you would probably expect me to be honest with you, and you might anticipate that what I have to say would

89

be a bit painful to hear. While Truth dreams can have this effect, more often dreams from Truth bring timely insight, hope, encouragement and power to you to become who you are supposed to be and to do what you are supposed to do.

If a dream is from Truth, it is often very vivid, and you do not have any problem remembering it. In *Dreams: A Documentary*, I interviewed a man who had been holding on to a dream for thirty years. He related it to me as if he had just dreamed it the previous night—it was that unforgettable to him. The ultimate purpose of dreams from Truth is to bring life and encouragement. A warning dream can be from Truth and may be sobering and shaking, but the goal is to save you from destruction. A warning dream says, "Wake up! You need to change direction or danger is on the way!" But it is a dream to awaken you to life, not death—to safety, not further harm.

Truth dreams give you a future and a hope. The purpose of a Truth dream is to make things right and set you free. Often, dreams from Truth will speak to you more than one time. These dreams will bring to light hidden things and give you answers, wisdom and guidance about how to handle a situation in your life.

Dreams from Truth propel you forward, get you unstuck from negative patterns and bring to light false views you have of yourself. They can bring healing from addictions or physical problems and provide creative ideas that lead to inventions. (We looked at a number of these dreams in chapter 1.) Truth dreams will launch you into your future in a good way. They will give you steps to take and direction about what to do with the message you have been given. Dreams from Truth—if interpreted properly—will give you hope and raise your expectations. Truth dreams often will cause you to see the reality of who or what you really are. This resonates with what you know to be true deep inside, and it causes you to start seeing yourself differently. As a result, you make changes in your life. These Truth dreams are often impossible to forget.

When an actress friend of mine started to pay attention to her dreams, she began to dream about parts of movies that she would be involved in. Not too long after this started, I was with her at a hotel. As we exited the lobby, the casting director for a major movie walked in. She knew him, and they struck up a conversation. He said he was going to send her a script for the movie—the one she had dreamed about. The dream had raised her expectations and put her on the lookout for this opportunity. The script fit her perfectly. This was a clear direction dream that God had intended for her, as she is a person who brings light and hope into the entertainment industry.

The Bible calls the Spirit of God the Spirit of Truth who will "guide you into all truth" (John 16:13). The Spirit of Truth will send you on a journey to seek out truth. The Spirit of Truth is compassionate and wants to bring positive change, not rub your nose in your problems and make you suffer. I encourage you to ask the Spirit of Truth to come and help you interpret your dreams. It is as simple as saying, "Spirit of Truth, help me understand this dream."

All of the dream themes in chapter 4 can come from the Spirit of Truth. No matter the dream, it is *your* dream. It is *your* encounter, and the Spirit of Truth will guide you into all truth, if you will ask. If you are not connected to the Spirit of Truth for your dream interpretation, a wrong interpretation is more likely. Before going to sleep, ask the Spirit of Truth to give you a dream from Truth. Just say, "Spirit of Truth, please give me a dream about truth in my life." The Spirit of Truth will indeed give you a dream if you want to come to grips with the truth and are willing to act on what is revealed. The fact that you are reading this book sets you up to know the truth and find it for yourself.

Let's practice determining the source of a dream. Earlier in this chapter, I asked you to turn to the dream journal at the back of this book and write down a dream you had that fit into one of the three categories I mentioned (the same dream recurring more than once; different dreams that have a similar theme; dreams that are so vivid, you feel as if you were there). Think about that dream, and if you have not written it down in the dream journal yet, do so now.

Based on what you have read so far, what do you think the source of that dream was—Self, Lie or Truth? Or was it a layer or a mix of sources? Write down your best guess. Remember that no matter the source of a dream, you can still gain information and benefit from the dream if you interpret it properly and flip it if needed.

Step 2: Determine the Message

Let's turn now to step two of dream interpretation—determine the message. When you are determining the message of your dreams, guard against overinterpretation, which can happen if you look only at the symbols in a dream. (See an example of this in the section titled "Online Dream Interpretation Site" at the end of the next chapter.) Also realize that since every dreamer is unique, an interpretation is going to be customized to the dreamer. While similar messages can be spoken to different people through dreams, I want you to take the time to search out what your dream is saying to you personally and what you can do about it.

Dreams are like a puzzle, and you will have to put together the pieces to arrive at an accurate meaning. At the opening of this chapter, I said that dream interpretation in its simplest form involves asking yourself, *What am I supposed to receive from this dream?* and *Why did I have this dream now?* Two additional questions that will help you determine the main message of your dream are these:

1. Am I Observing or Participating?

When you are *observing* in a dream, you could take yourself out of it and the events in the dream could still happen. The dream is not about you. If you are observing, you are being shown something that may or may not require action. Ask yourself why you are being

92

shown this dream. Is there any action you need to take? Or is the dream just something that has not happened yet that you now have knowledge of? Are you being shown something that to date has been unsolvable? Your dream may be saying that you will come to a crossroads where you need to make a decision about something, and through the dream, you are seeing what is going on before you have to make the decision. If the dream is just providing knowledge, be careful that you do not get involved in someone's life where they do not want you or where you have not been invited.

When you are *participating* in a dream, the actions in the dream could not happen without you. You could not take yourself out of it and have the events unfold the same way. When you are participating, then the dream usually has something to do with you personally or with your involvement in a situation or event.

2. What Is the Main Element or Focus?

Consider which of the following is the main element or focus of the dream: a person, an object or image, a situation or the timing.

Person: If the main focus or object in the dream is a person (other than yourself), ask yourself how you know them or how they are related to you. Dreams often contain symbolic language, so the person may be a picture of something in your life and may not necessarily represent himself or herself.

For example, my friend Dave dreamed that he and his brother were riding bikes together, but his brother was riding a bike that was way too small. His brother began to show off and do tricks as if he were a real hot shot, which seemed completely out of place since he was riding an elementary student's bicycle. The dream was not about Dave's brother literally, but about how we as "brothers and sisters" can be arrogant about our abilities without realizing that we still have not passed an "elementary" level.

Object: If the main focus of the dream is an object, ask yourself what that object has to do with you and how you feel about it. Earlier in this book, I shared the true story of Floyd Ragsdale, an engineer with no college education who solved an engineering problem by acting on a dream. On another occasion he had a dream about troubleshooting a filter on a machine. In the dream, he was working next to a man who was sweating profusely. The man passed out and then died. A person walked by and said, "We've got to get a pacemaker to revive him." When Ragsdale woke up, he wrote down the word *pacemaker*. Later he began to think about how a pacemaker related to the problem with the machine. Ragsdale talked to an electrician, who was able to produce a timer box for the filter. It solved the problem and saved the company hundreds of thousands of dollars.[1]

Keep in mind that an object in a dream can mean one thing to one person and something totally different to someone else. If you were to ask me what a swimming pool means in your dream, I would reply, "I don't know. What was happening in your dream? Were you in the pool? Was it in public or in your backyard? What do swimming pools mean to you? Are they a refreshing place, or are they a scary place because you almost drowned when you were young?" You can see that an object can mean different things to different people.

Situation or event: If the focus of the dream is a situation or event, ask yourself how what is going on in your life might be related to the dream, and also what wisdom can be drawn from the dream to apply to that situation.

I had a dream just before our team was getting ready to interpret dreams at an event none of us had ever been to before. This event was especially important because we were building a dream team that would return annually. In this dream, I was with some other people on a medium-sized fishing boat. This boat had a small, box-like glass enclosure in the middle, near the steering wheel. From a distance we could see a huge tidal wave forming. Our boat was still in calm water, but we observed a boat that looked like the *Titanic* trying to go over the top of the wave. The boat was extremely high as it proceeded to crest the gigantic wave. I could see the steam rise from the five smokestacks as it tried to slow itself down on the backside of the wave. I knew in the dream that this boat would not successfully complete the task and would ultimately hit the bottom of the wave and crash, bow first, into the sea.

All of the sudden, our fishing vessel was faced with the same challenge, except as we approached the wave, the bow of our boat entered into the base of the wave and we were submerged in water. Our team of dream interpreters was inside the glass box on the boat as we continued through the bottom swell of the wave. Suddenly, we popped out on the other side. I looked down at my hand, and I had my cell phone in it. I was able to phone ahead to other boats facing the same challenge and tell them how to get through the seemingly overwhelming situation to reach a successful end.

The timing of this dream and the instruction I received caused me to feel confident about immersing myself in the culture of the place where we were going. Although it was very different from anything any of us had previously experienced, I knew our efforts would be welcome and would open the door for an invitation to return in years to come.

Timing: Sometimes the main focus of a dream is the timing— the urgency of action needed or specific timing to keep in mind. A recurring dream about something in your past may point to the fact that you have not dealt with an important issue; it keeps showing its face so you will deal with it and move on. The timing in a dream is sometimes as important as the dream itself, and being aware of timing will help you address the issues in the right season. It will also help you get to where you need to be, when you need to be there.

A friend of mine had a dream about her earthly father giving her a watch. She took it in her hand and opened the cover; then the same watch appeared in the sky. As she looked at the time, the earth began to shake and give way underneath the place where the watch was up in the sky.

Let's break down this dream. First, the dream was about her and the message she was given. She was a participant because if you had taken her out of the dream, it would not have happened. She was the one who was given the watch, and where would it have gone without her?

The secondary element was the watch itself. It was also important that it was her father who gave it to her—someone who was 95 years old at the time was saying in essence, "I may not be here when this happens, but it's important for me to instruct you now. When you see this timing, things could happen very quickly."

The third element was the instability and crisis of the land. In this dream, she knew that her earthly father was giving her a message having to do with the timing of an event that would radically change her life and the lives of those around her. When the ground gives way in a dream, another foundation is getting ready to be created. This foundation will be a supportive pathway and will give others a place to build their lives on that will not crumble when times on the earth are out of their control.

This dream obviously got my friend's attention. She realized that she was being given responsibility over the timing of an important event, but also that she needed to "watch" and understand that situations of shaking and unrest were ahead in the future.

While this last example contains a number of elements in the dream (a wise *father* giving instructions to *watch* for *shaking* and be prepared), remember to keep it simple when you search out the message of a dream. How do you keep it simple, especially if your dream contains a number of elements, yet get it right? Ask the Spirit of Truth, "What is the main point of this dream?" and then go with that. Walking away with something small is better than walking away with nothing at all.

Step 3: Determine Your Response

We have looked at determining the source of a dream and determining its message. The third step is determining your response. How you respond to your dreams is an important part of the dream interpretation process. Dreams show you something you need to pay attention to, and they are often a call to action.

A *dream* may unlock a solution, but your *response* is what puts that solution into action for your benefit and the benefit of others. I hope the dream stories I have shared so far in this book have encouraged you. They show what happens when a dreamer responds in some way to his or her dream. Diabetics live today because Frederick Banting responded to his dream. The world wears Nike shoes (and not Dimension 6) because Jeff Johnson suggested the name he saw in his dream to his bosses. Students read books by Robert Louis Stevenson and Mary Shelley because they wrote stories based on their dreams.

Dreams can be "prophetic" in nature, foretelling future events. However, just because you have a dream does not necessarily mean it will come to pass. You need to act on it, like Banting, Johnson, Stevenson, Shelley and others I have mentioned. A proper response is especially important if your dream is warning you about a potential danger ahead. In this case, the purpose of your dream is not to foretell an inevitable future event, but to help you *avoid* it, or at a minimum, lessen its impact.

If you are really into dreams, you may be tempted to act on every dream you have. But sometimes the only response that is needed is to "park" a dream, write it down so you do not forget it, maybe chew on it for a while, but also realize that it might not be the right time to take action on it. Sometimes some life needs to be lived before you are supposed to act on what you have been shown in a dream. Timing is important if you are being called to action. Regardless, you need to take action of some kind to implement the solution your dream is providing you.

A Few Extras

A few other things to consider as you interpret dreams are what to do with a dream within a dream or a vision within a dream. If you have a dream within a dream, start with the dream you are dreaming first, then interpret the complete dream. The dream you are dreaming within a dream is a message you are being given that has to do with the outside dream. In the movie *Inception*, Leonardo DiCaprio's character, Dom Cobb, has a dream within a dream within a dream within a dream. I was intrigued as I watched the movie because once I determined that there were four dreams, I was able to follow the storyline in the movie much better.

Take a similar approach to a vision within a dream. I believe that this is what Joseph, Jesus' earthly father, had when the angel appeared to him in a dream and gave him instructions. The angel brought a clear message that needed no interpretation. (See Matthew 1:18–25.) While dreams contain symbols, visions often do not. What you see is what you get, so visions usually do not need a detailed interpretation.

Do not get caught up in trying to figure out if you have had a dream within a dream or a vision within a dream, though. The point here is that sometimes there is more going on than you think, but the goal remains the same—to understand the basic message and respond to it in some way.

Although dreaming can be fun, dreaming is not a game. A dream is a powerful tool in the hand of a person who can interpret it properly and take appropriate action. At the simplest level, if you want to know how to interpret your dreams, just remember to think about the source (Self, Lie or Truth), write down the main message you think is being given and do something in response to the dream—even if it is small. The more faithful you are to respond to your dreams, the more you will be given.

TAKEAWAYS

- There are three main steps to dream interpretation: Determine the source, determine the message and determine your response.

- Keep dream interpretation simple. It is better to be able to act on a simple, accurate interpretation than to have the message remain a mystery while you try to figure out the meaning down to every last detail.

- Learn how to flip a seemingly bad dream so that no matter what the source of your dream, you can understand what is really going on and make the dream work for you and not against you.

7

REINTERPRETING DREAMS

Situation: A friend was wondering if she should add chicken and protein to a special juicing diet she had implemented for cancer treatment.

Dream: She dreamed that I was in her kitchen with a blue ice chest that had a white lid. Inside the ice chest were two frozen chickens in Safeway wrappers (Safeway is the name of a U.S. grocery story chain). I told my friend that these chickens were hers, not mine, and that she had bought them and should take them. At first she did not think she should, but I told her they had been kept very cold and were unspoiled, so she decided to take them and put them in her freezer.

Solution: Her dream showed her that adding chicken to her diet was okay and a "safe way" to eat now. She began to incorporate chicken into her diet.

This chapter includes the dreams of some famous and not-so-famous people. I have taken these dreams from just a couple of the many dream interpretation websites. If you are new to dream interpretation, you will discover that it is quite popular, and I think it is helpful to see how others interpret dreams and how varied the interpretations can be that emerge as a result.

In the following pages, I will include the dreams themselves, the initial interpretation, and my alternate interpretation. As you read, think about how *you* would have interpreted these dreams and what kind of solutions the various interpretations provide for the dreamer.

Dream by Kristen Bell—American Actress

I once had a dream that happened quite a few times, where my dog fell apart like a hot dog and I had to put him back together with toothpicks.[1]

Original Interpretation

Assuming this came during childhood, it's another example of an existential problem that children sometimes find themselves confronting in their dreams. At some point in early life, whether from an actual loss or a vivid nightmare like this, children discover the ultimate frailty of life and the fact that all we know and love will eventually fall apart and die. I would say the dream means nothing more or less than, "This is the way life is."

Perhaps this person has experienced similar dreams or nightmares when suffering losses later in life. The mourning process might bring back some of these childhood feelings of vulnerability.[2]

Cindy McGill Reinterpretation

Assuming this person loved her dog, the dream had something to do with someone or something she loved and cared for. Since this was a recurring dream, it had to do with relationships or things important to her that fell apart during her life at that time, but that she did not know how to fix or put back together again.

She cared a great deal, but the situation was out of her control. It was not her responsibility to fix the situation, and when she tried, the result was a feeble attempt that did not hold. Maybe it was her family or her parents who fell apart, and she felt responsible to put their family relationships back together, but she could not. Some things have to be given over to a higher power to fix.

It is interesting to note that this person experienced many situations growing up where things fell apart, and it is easy to see how she would try to put them back together. This includes her parents' divorce when she was two, having to relate to two half sisters and four stepsiblings, not liking her name, having strabismus that affected her right eye, changing schools and dealing with the death of her best friend.[3] (I include these personal facts about Bell here to give insight into the possible meaning behind her dream, but note that I did not know any of this information when I reinterpreted her dream. In fact, for all of the following dreams, the dreamers' identities were unknown to me when I did the reinterpretations.) Think about how it would have empowered her to know during these years that she was not responsible to fix these "broken" things, but could look to a higher, stronger power for strength and hope.

Dream by Ray Winstone—English Film and Television Actor

I was standing under a huge tree—it must have been on the Serengeti, somewhere in Africa—and I was watching my family being eaten by lions. I had that dream over and over again when I was a kid . . . I'm guessing it came from some programme I saw on the telly. For that reason I've never been to Africa and I would never take my family there. Even now I'm . . . scared of lions and when I go to the zoo I get the feeling that they can smell me and they're plotting to get me. I'll tell you how ridiculous my fear of them is: my daughter had to go to South Africa last year to do a film and I was begging her not to go. Because of the lions.[4]

Original Interpretation

One can imagine exactly the same nightmare being experienced by our human ancestors thousands of years ago, when they actually lived on the Serengeti and had to worry about real lions attacking them. The instinctual imprint of that fear still echoes in the dreams of people today. A TV show might spark it, but the unconscious mind is already primed to raise the alarm. Even if they seem out of place in modern society, even if they seem entirely foolish and unreasonable, these hard-wired instincts still shape our perceptions of possible dangers in the world.

There might be something more to the symbolism of the lions for this dreamer, perhaps having to do with family aggression or masculine authority. The persistence of this fear from a childhood dream into adulthood makes me wonder if this is a person who, for better or for worse, puts great trust in his instincts and gut-level reactions.[5]

Cindy McGill Reinterpretation

Lions typically have two meanings in dreams. A lion can either represent an honorable king, which is good if you are a law-abiding follower, or a predator, which is bad if you are the prey. If this person had this dream over and over as a kid, the lion had something to do with a force in his generational line. As a predator, it may have referred to something that was threatening to take over or destroy him and his family. The good part was that he was being given an opportunity to deal with it. He could break this power over his family because he was the one who was entrusted with the dream.

This person may not have realized all that as a child, of course, but part of my reason for sharing this is to teach parents not to ignore their children's dreams. Children can find solutions in their dreams, too, if parents will help them overcome their fears and sort through the meaning. This dream was a warning that an enemy or a negative force in the family line was trying to keep them from fulfilling their destiny or potential. It was also an encouragement to remove this predator before it took his family captive or destroyed them. This person was given an opportunity to face this "lion" instead of living in fear. Facing the predator would have a positive outcome for him and his family.

It is important to note that this enemy would not have bothered trailing the family if there were not something important to go after or if the family did not have strong potential that the enemy wanted to stop. This dream was given not to instill fear, but so that the dreamer could turn and face his enemy and overcome it.

Dream by Samuel L. Jackson—American Film and Television Actor and Film Producer

I have this dream about falling all the time. People say that if you ever hit the ground in a falling dream you'll have a heart attack and die. So I try to stay with the dream and see what happens. I've actually fallen from very high distances, hit the ground, gone through and ended up in water. But I can still breathe and finally end up in air again. Then I start flying. It's a very cool dream; I kind of look forward to it now.[6]

Original Interpretation

To actually die in a dream, rather than waking up just a moment before death, is indeed unusual. When it occurs it tends to be very memorable and thought-provoking.

One of the general functions of dreaming is to expand our conscious sense of possibility and keep our minds flexible, adaptive, and open to alternative perspectives. In this case the dreamer pushes the process further than most people are willing to go. In many religious traditions these would be considered mystical experiences, and the dreamer might be taken aside for special training as a healer or shaman.

Some research has suggested that people who can guide their dreams like this have better physical balance and spatial coordination in waking life. Perhaps this dreamer is a dancer or an athlete of some kind?[7]

Cindy McGill Reinterpretation

In this dream, this person falls from a great height, goes through water and ends up in water, yet he can still breathe and ends up flying in the air. This dream is showing that he is breaking barriers on both levels. It tells me something about his destiny and also about his character. He is designed to break barriers, go distances and do things others have not done, yet he never loses his ability to breathe. He thrives or flies through the whole experience and can break barriers in both the "high" and the "deep."

A quick review of Jackson's accomplishments shows that he has lived a life of breaking barriers and going higher and deeper than those around him. (Remember, though, that I did these reinterpretations without knowing the identity of the dreamer.) Jackson grew up in the tumultuous South, persevering through attending several segregated schools. He was also deeply involved in the conflict of the civil rights movement. The 2009 edition of the *Guinness World Records* also states that Jackson is the world's highest-grossing actor, having earned $7.42 billion in 68 films.[8] That is definitely flying high!

Dream by Kate Winslet—English Actress and Singer

When I was a kid, we had lots of hamsters. And one of them suddenly gave birth; we didn't even know she was pregnant. We phoned the pet shop and they said, "Take the babies away—hamsters get very frightened after they've given birth and you don't want her to eat the babies." We didn't listen and that's exactly what happened: the babies just disappeared. This obviously affected me badly as I had a recurring dream about hamsters gobbling up babies until I was about 15. And that's the reason why I will never again be able to keep a pet hamster, gerbil or mouse![9]

Original Interpretation

Although they were probably never diagnosed as such, these dreams fit the bill of post-traumatic nightmares. Studies of PTSD suggest that people who have suffered traumas in the past are more vulnerable when new traumas occur, so perhaps this person has higher risk factors in that regard.

The specific image is both mundane and mythic. Many people in modern society have grown up with pet rodents as an ordinary part of childhood life. But the horrifying act of a mother devouring her young is a primordial theme of mythology echoed in frightening stories about the Hindu goddess Kali and the witch in Hansel and Gretel. No wonder the hamster carnage was so disturbing!

Depending on the dreamer's relationship to her own mother, the recurrence of these dreams might reflect personal fears about her mother's potentially devouring role in her life.

It is interesting that the dreams ended at 15, with the onset of adolescence and reproductive maturity. Perhaps the emergence of the dreamer's own maternal power and generative potential gave her the strength to break the nightmare spell of the evil mother.[10]

Cindy McGill Reinterpretation

This dreamer hates injustice, especially when it comes to things that endanger the weak and helpless. Babies are something you nurture. If you are pregnant in a dream and not pregnant in real life, then you have been given responsibility over birthing and raising something—a job, a relationship or whatever.

In her personal life, this person has some sort of anxiety over missed opportunities or things that were not nurtured or cared for properly—things that had life, but got eaten up. This dream goes deeper than hamsters or babies. Something was born and then not given the chance to live, and seeing that spurred in her a desire for justice. It is possible that at the time, life dreams or aspirations were forming in her about her future, and she was facing some fear that those would never play out—would never be given the chance to live.

She also chose not to have the kind of pets in the dream again, which could indicate that in other areas of her life she may also choose to avoid loss.

Dream by Judd Apatow—American Film Producer, Director and Screenwriter

I've had a lot of incredibly vivid aircraft-out-of-control-about-to-crash dreams. You know, when you wake up and it feels like it happened. A lot of airplanes narrowly avoiding things, coming down fast. I'm never flying the plane—I'm always freaking out in the back.[11]

Original Interpretation

Nightmares like this plague many people in modern society. Most of us feel some degree of anxiety about air travel, however successful we are at masking it. Terrifying plane-crashing dreams seem to be Nature's way of protesting against our jet-setting lifestyles.

Plane crash dreams can be rather obvious symbols of a fear of "falling," whether in one's career, relationships, or personal behavior (perhaps in reference to sobriety?). The dreams don't necessarily mean the person actually *has* fallen in waking life, just that the *danger* of falling is something the person worries about a great deal.

These dreams might be a good opportunity to practice what Jung called "active imagination." It involves closing one's eyes and reentering the dream—but instead of staying in the back, the person could try going up to the cockpit and taking control of the plane. The results of this imaginal experiment might be surprising![12]

Cindy McGill Reinterpretation

This dream has to do with opportunities or projects that have come to this person and shows that he does not trust those involved with him to "fly" or to direct things correctly. His life or an important part of his existence is in jeopardy because he is "on the plane" or is connected with these people in some significant way. The dream could be about his career and the people with whom he is connected. It shows that he has fears about who is in control. He is in the back of the plane, which tells me that he feels he is not in control the way he would be if he were in the driver's seat.

At the time of these dreams, this person was probably feeling as though he was connected to people who did not know what they were doing. They were taking chances with his career and coming down fast, narrowly avoiding disaster. This could be a warning dream to go instead with other people he trusts who are safer. This dream could also be showing his need to be in control of his own destiny.

Online Dream Interpretation

The following dream, which I find quite profound, is a paraphrase of a dream that was posted on an Internet dream sharing and interpretation site. On this site, people can enter a dream into a "Dream Interpreter." After people submit a dream, they can click on a "Dream Interpretation" button, which then gives a compilation of the dream language meanings of all the key words underlined in the dream. Underlined words are links to a generic dream language database where the meaning of each underlined word is given. (You will see what I mean when we get to the original interpretation of the dream, which was given on the website. I have underlined some words in the dream below as an example.) How would you interpret this dream?

A girl dreamed that she was in an unknown town with her mother and grandmother. A baby had been stolen, and she was running around looking for it with her grandma and her mom, but she knew they did not really care about the baby. They found out the baby was in a parking garage, so she ran as fast as she could to get there, while the other two women took a longer route by car. She arrived to find two men looking for the baby, but she found the little baby girl first in a garbage bin. She jumped inside the trash with the baby to hide it, and she called the police. When it was safe she picked up the baby, only to discover that the baby was she herself![13]

Interpretation from the Website

Some of the words the website underlined in this person's dream description were *mom, town, baby, stolen, running, looking, grandmother, jumped, car, found, guys, garbage, hide* and *discover*—49 words total in the online version of her dream. Since the interpretation for this dream is eight pages long online, I will only include what the site stated for a few of these words, *town, baby, stolen* and *running*, so you can see what interpreting a dream using only symbols is like.

The site says that a *town* represents restrictions. It can also represent being unsophisticated, yet well-balanced and community oriented. A *baby* on the site has a number of meanings. It can mean the dreamer needs to cater to his or her inner self. A related item like an empty baby carriage can indicate an unfulfilled goal or the desire to have children. The site says the image of something being *stolen* indicates that the dreamer has been robbed or is experiencing some sort of loss or identity crisis. It may also signify that someone else has stolen the dreamer's success. *Running* indicates that the dreamer has worries about health or beauty or fitting in. It may also indicate a dreamer's need to exercise his or her rights and power in some situation.

And so on for every word that is underlined in the text of a dream. The dreamer then can piece together the meaning of his or her dream from the key word symbols that come up as a result. Visitors to the site can view, rate and comment on other people's dreams if they want to. Many of the dreams have great depth of meaning and wonderful potential to help the dreamer. But most dreams have no comments, so people who post a dream are for the most part on their own when figuring out the meaning using the "Dream Interpreter" tool.

Cindy McGill Reinterpretation

Basically, this dreamer interpreted her own dream. Her life felt valueless, and her mother and grandmother seemed to reinforce her negative shortcomings. But at the time of the dream, this person is at a point in her life when she is taking back her own destiny. The baby represents her, and although the people who should have nurtured her discarded her instead, she is on the hunt to take charge of her life and make something of it.

Parking garages are places where there is no movement because everything is "parked." In this girl's case, her potential is "parked" here, but so is her memory and realization of what her destiny really is. This dream tells me that this young girl has great potential. Because of this girl's fight within to take charge of the "baby"—herself—she likely will go on to accomplish just about anything she sets her mind to. A direct attempt to sabotage her life was made from the onset because of the voice this girl has and the effect she will have for good on this earth. I love this dream.

Interpretation Is Unique

Every person is unique, and as I have shared previously, dreams are personal and come in a language that is meaningful to the dreamer. We can compare common symbols that appear in dreams from person to person, but the key is to get the whole picture—not only the dream, but also what is going on in the person's life.

In my journey with dream interpretation teams in many countries and on the streets of cities large and small, we have talked to many people who have had a disturbing dream and have afterward gone to a bookstore, found a dream symbols book and tried to find the hidden meaning of their dream without much accuracy or success. After such a person tells our team his or her dream, however, the whole picture comes alive and we are able not only to speak to the dream the person had, but also to suggest how it can be applied to his or her life.

As you think about your dreams, remember that an accurate interpretation will leave you with insight that brings you strength to move into a better place in life. If that is not the case with the original interpretation of your dream, the dream may need to be reinterpreted.

TAKEAWAYS

- Do not try to interpret your dreams using their symbols only.
- Ask yourself the questions I have suggested in this book to determine an accurate interpretation of your dream.
- An accurate dream interpretation will provide insight and a solution that moves you into a better place in life.

8

WHEN GOD GIVES A DREAM

Situation: I had just made a job change. Previously, I had
worked on developing new ideas and products for my former employer.

Dream: I dreamed that I received a letter from someone.
What was unusual about the letter was that the words
were cut out from headlines in different magazines (what
a ransom note might look like) and put together to create
the message. The dream showed this letter arriving and
tempting me to be fearful. Instead, I was calm.

Solution: Within a few days of the dream, my former employer really did mail me a letter claiming that he had
rights to my ideas and threatening to take everything I
owned. He also threatened to prevent me from working
in the development field. I was relieved, knowing God
had given me advance notice of this attack. I was able to
stay calm because I knew God was in control and would
help me.

Thousands of years ago, ancient Egyptians used the messages in
their dreams to cure illnesses, make important state decisions,

determine where to build religious structures and decide when to wage a battle. Dreams were considered divine predictions of the future.[1]

The Bible, a reliable source of ancient manuscripts and events, records dreams that have played a significant role in history. In this chapter, we will look at a number of dreams given to government leaders or rulers as recorded in the Bible.

A Boy Who Became a Ruler

Joseph was the eleventh son of Jacob, and Jacob was the grandson of Abraham, who is considered the father of Judaism, Christianity and Islam. Later in life, Jacob's name was changed to Israel, from which the nation of Israel derived its name. Joseph received a gift as a boy: dreams from God. But this gift was neither received nor appreciated by his family—especially by his brothers, who were jealous of him. Genesis 37:5–11 documents the dreams Joseph had when he was seventeen years old:

> Now Joseph had a dream, and he told it to his brothers; and they hated him even more. So he said to them, "Please hear this dream which I have dreamed: There we were, binding sheaves in the field. Then behold, my sheaf arose and also stood upright; and indeed your sheaves stood all around and bowed down to my sheaf."
>
> And his brothers said to him, "Shall you indeed reign over us? Or shall you indeed have dominion over us?" So they hated him even more for his dreams and for his words.
>
> Then he dreamed still another dream and told it to his brothers, and said, "Look, I have dreamed another dream. And this time, the sun, the moon, and the eleven stars bowed down to me."
>
> So he told it to his father and his brothers; and his father rebuked him and said to him, "What is this dream that you have dreamed? Shall your mother and I and your brothers indeed come to bow down to the earth before you?" And his brothers envied him, but his father kept the matter in mind.

This dream foretold a time when Joseph's family would literally bow before him. He would be a ruler in Egypt thirteen years later, but none of them could possibly imagine that at the time of his dreams. When Joseph shared his dreams about his destiny, his brothers were so enraged that they sold him to some traders passing by. Joseph ended up in Egypt as a slave in an Egyptian officer's house. The officer's wife made a play for Joseph, and when Joseph refused her advances, she falsely accused him of rape—which got him thrown in prison. Welcome to Egypt, Joseph.

Joseph found himself in prison, but even there he demonstrated such good character that he was put in charge over all that went on inside the prison and over the prisoners themselves. Joseph would eventually realize that his time in prison was preparation for leadership. He could not have handled the responsibility he was going to walk in later without it. Later in life, he would say to his brothers, "But as for you, you meant evil against me; but God meant it for good, in order to bring it about as it is this day, to save many people alive" (Genesis 50:20).

But for now, Joseph was a prisoner. During this time, the king's chief butler and baker offended their master and got thrown in prison. The captain of the guard assigned them to Joseph, and Joseph took care of them. After they had been in custody for a time, they both had a dream on the same night. When Joseph went to take care of their needs the next morning, he saw that their faces were sad and asked what was going on.

"We both had dreams," they answered, "but there is no one to interpret them" (Genesis 40:8 NIV). Without an Internet connection or access to the psychic network outside the prison, they were at a loss.

But Joseph said, "Do not interpretations belong to God? Tell me your dreams" (verse 8). So the chief butler related his dream, and Joseph interpreted it:

"Behold, in my dream a vine was before me, and in the vine were three branches; it was as though it budded, its blossoms shot forth, and its clusters brought forth ripe grapes. Then Pharaoh's cup was in my hand; and I took the grapes and pressed them into Pharaoh's cup, and placed the cup in Pharaoh's hand."

And Joseph said to him, "This is the interpretation of it: The three branches are three days. Now within three days Pharaoh will lift up your head and restore you to your place, and you will put Pharaoh's cup in his hand according to the former manner, when you were his butler."

Genesis 40:9–13

If we look more closely at this dream, we can see that every element in it contained life. There was life in the vine, life in the blossoms and life in the grapes. Then the butler returned the cup into Pharaoh's hand, which speaks of restoration. The butler got some good news from his dream. He would be restored to his position, and life would be good once again.

When the baker saw that the butler's dream had a good interpretation, he also told Joseph his dream, and Joseph interpreted it:

"I also was in my dream, and there were three white baskets on my head. In the uppermost basket were all kinds of baked goods for Pharaoh, and the birds ate them out of the basket on my head."

So Joseph answered and said, "This is the interpretation of it: The three baskets are three days. Within three days Pharaoh will lift off your head from you and hang you on a tree; and the birds will eat your flesh from you."

Verses 16–19

Gulp. Who would want to give a person an interpretation like that? "Oh, by the way, you're going to die and it's going to be gruesome!" But in his dream, things were being stripped away from the baker. The birds were taking the bread. Because bread was made every day for the king, three baskets represented three days. That is how Joseph was able to understand the hidden meaning of this dream.

Everything came true for both the butler and the baker, just as Joseph had said. After interpreting the butler's dream, Joseph had said to him,

> But remember me when it is well with you, and please show kindness to me; make mention of me to Pharaoh, and get me out of this house. For indeed I was stolen away from the land of the Hebrews; and also I have done nothing here that they should put me into the dungeon.
>
> Verses 14–15

Unfortunately, the butler forgot about Joseph and two years went by. I would like to pause in the middle of this story to make a few important points. If you are a dreamer (remember, we all dream) and you have also been given a gift of dream interpretation, it is not going to go away. Keep in mind that Joseph had to wait a long time for his gift to work to his benefit, and until that time, his gift worked against him. If you find yourself in a difficult place, as Joseph did, do not despise your perceived prison.

People always want to know why they are going through hard stuff. This is why: Hard stuff is preparation for where you are headed—if you will allow the preparation process to have its full effect. Maybe your time has not yet arrived because either you are not ready or the place you are moving to is not ready for you. Right now, your life may not be what you expected or what you have striven to achieve, but if you will allow God to direct your life and prepare you for where you are going, you will go farther than you ever dreamed possible. Where you end up will be greater than anything you could have imagined.

Joseph had every reason to stuff his dreams and his gift. Facing the challenges that met him along his way, he had a choice to make—whether to get bitter or get better. Either way, the gift was not leaving him. So when the butler and baker had dreams, he used his gift again, even after it had gotten him into so much trouble with his family.

Two years later, the interpretation Joseph provided for the butler would pay off. Pharaoh, the ruler of Egypt, had two dreams with the same message, and his dreams haunted him. (The two dreams had different elements, but the message was the same.) Genesis 41:1–7 records these dreams:

> Then it came to pass, at the end of two full years, that Pharaoh had a dream; and behold, he stood by the river. Suddenly there came up out of the river seven cows, fine looking and fat; and they fed in the meadow. Then behold, seven other cows came up after them out of the river, ugly and gaunt, and stood by the other cows on the bank of the river. And the ugly and gaunt cows ate up the seven fine looking and fat cows. So Pharaoh awoke. He slept and dreamed a second time; and suddenly seven heads of grain came up on one stalk, plump and good. Then behold, seven thin heads, blighted by the east wind, sprang up after them. And the seven thin heads devoured the seven plump and full heads. So Pharaoh awoke, and indeed, it was a dream.

In the morning Pharaoh could not shake the dreams, and they troubled him. He called for all the magicians and wise men of Egypt (the psychics and dream interpreters of that day) and told them his dreams, but no one could interpret them. Then the chief butler spoke up and told Pharaoh about Joseph, whom he had met in prison, saying, "Now there was a young Hebrew man with us there . . . and he interpreted our dreams for us; to each man he interpreted according to his own dream. And it came to pass, just as he interpreted for us" (Genesis 41:12–13). So Pharaoh sent for Joseph, and here is what transpired:

> They brought him quickly out of the dungeon; and he shaved, changed his clothing, and came to Pharaoh. And Pharaoh said to

Joseph, "I have had a dream, and there is no one who can interpret it. But I have heard it said of you that you can understand a dream, to interpret it."

So Joseph answered Pharaoh, saying, "It is not in me; God will give Pharaoh an answer of peace."

Genesis 41:14–16

Note that the correct interpretation of a dream brings "peace." Pharaoh told Joseph his dream, and then Joseph said to Pharaoh,

The dreams of Pharaoh are one; God has shown Pharaoh what He is about to do: The seven good cows are seven years, and the seven good heads are seven years; the dreams are one. And the seven thin and ugly cows which came up after them are seven years, and the seven empty heads blighted by the east wind are seven years of famine. This is the thing which I have spoken to Pharaoh. God has shown Pharaoh what He is about to do. Indeed seven years of great plenty will come throughout all the land of Egypt; but after them seven years of famine will arise, and all the plenty will be forgotten in the land of Egypt; and the famine will deplete the land. So the plenty will not be known in the land because of the famine following, for it will be very severe. And the dream was repeated to Pharaoh twice because the thing is established by God, and God will shortly bring it to pass.

Verses 25–32

Let me summarize this incredible dream story. Pharaoh has a couple of dreams and is troubled because he knows they are sending him an important message. He goes to different people to get the interpretation and no one can help, but then he finds the proper interpretation in a young man who knows that dreams come from God and that the right interpretation can only be found with God's help.

In both of Pharaoh's dreams, the scrawny eat up the fat. Joseph knows that seven represented seven years, and the reason Pharaoh knows Joseph's interpretation is correct is because it resonates with him. In *Dreams: A Documentary*, you can see this same response when we share an accurate interpretation with someone. The interpretation sits well with the dreamer, and he or she knows it is an accurate interpretation—it answers a question and is the right key to unlocking a mystery.

Joseph gives Pharaoh the interpretation, and overnight he becomes the second-most-powerful ruler in the world. Joseph is put in charge of Egypt when he is thirty years old—after enduring thirteen years of hardship before seeing his dreams come true. But Joseph sees them come to pass; he had just told them to the wrong people at the wrong time initially. That just goes to show that sometimes it is good to hang on to secrets revealed in dreams.

Let this story about Joseph give you the strength to get through any dungeon you find yourself in right now. Just because you have not seen your promotion yet does not mean there is no future for you. Most likely, your future is greater than you ever could imagine, and it will come to pass if you will make the most of your prison and let it be your preparation until your breakthrough comes.

A Ruler Who Became an Animal

Nebuchadnezzar the Great lived from 634–562 BC and ruled over one of the most powerful periods in Babylonian history. He is known for building the Hanging Gardens of Babylon, one of the seven wonders of the ancient world. He also conquered Syria and Egypt (a rare and amazing feat) and destroyed the Temple of Solomon in Jerusalem, sending many Jews into exile.

The Bible contains two detailed accounts of this ancient leader's dreams. These historical events are a remarkable case study of a leader who received clear direction and warning dreams from God and what happened as a result. The accounts give clear evidence that God sends dreams to guide and warn world leaders, regardless of their religious loyalties. Let's take a look at these amazing dreams.

The Rise and Fall of World Powers

King Nebuchadnezzar had only been on the throne for a couple of years when he was given a dream so astounding in its scope that it covered the rise and fall of world powers from the time of his rule until the rule of a Kingdom at the end of time. It is no wonder that trying to figure out its meaning worried him and kept him awake at night! He called together all the magicians, astrologers, sorcerers and wise men in the kingdom to help him sort out the dream.

The king must have thought that interpreting the dream would be too easy for these guys—they could make up anything once they heard it. But he was looking for accuracy, so he demanded that the dream interpreters tell him not only the interpretation, but also the actual dream itself. If they could not, he threatened that he would give the order to cut them to pieces and burn down their houses. Terrified by the king's unusual demand, his interpreters replied,

> There is not a man on earth who can tell the king's matter; therefore no king, lord, or ruler has ever asked such things of any magician, astrologer, or Chaldean. It is a difficult thing that the king requests, and there is no other who can tell it to the king except the gods, whose dwelling is not with flesh.
>
> Daniel 2:10–11

Infuriated by their reply, the king ordered the captain of the guard to proceed with their executions. When the captain tracked down Daniel (one of the wise men) to kill him, Daniel asked, "Why is the decree from the king so urgent?" (verse 15). The captain filled him in and then allowed him to approach the king to ask for more time. The king granted his request, so Daniel and his companions began to seek God for the answers required to save their lives. God answered their prayers and revealed the secret to Daniel in a night vision. Daniel then went to tell the king both the dream itself and also its interpretation:

You, O king, were watching; and behold, a great image! This great image, whose splendor was excellent, stood before you; and its form was awesome. This image's head was of fine gold, its chest and arms of silver, its belly and thighs of bronze, its legs of iron, its feet partly of iron and partly of clay. You watched while a stone was cut out without hands, which struck the image on its feet of iron and clay, and broke them in pieces. Then the iron, the clay, the bronze, the silver, and the gold were crushed together, and became like chaff from the summer threshing floors; the wind carried them away so that no trace of them was found. And the stone that struck the image became a great mountain and filled the whole earth.

This is the dream. Now we will tell the interpretation of it before the king. You, O king, are a king of kings. For the God of heaven has given you a kingdom, power, strength, and glory; and wherever the children of men dwell, or the beasts of the field and the birds of the heaven, He has given them into your hand, and has made you ruler over them all—you are this head of gold. But after you shall arise another kingdom inferior to yours; then another, a third kingdom of bronze, which shall rule over all the earth. And the fourth kingdom shall be as strong as iron, inasmuch as iron breaks in pieces and shatters everything; and like iron that crushes, that kingdom will break in pieces and crush all the others. Whereas you saw the feet and toes, partly of potter's clay and partly of iron, the kingdom shall be divided; yet the strength of the iron shall be in it, just as you saw the iron mixed with ceramic clay. And as the toes of the feet were partly of iron and partly of clay, so the kingdom shall be partly strong and partly fragile. As you saw iron mixed with ceramic clay, they will mingle with the seed of men; but they will not adhere to one another, just as iron does not mix with clay. And in the days of these kings the God of heaven will set up a kingdom which shall never be destroyed; and the kingdom shall not be left to other people; it shall break in pieces and consume all these kingdoms, and it shall stand forever. Inasmuch as you saw that the stone was cut out of the mountain without hands, and that it broke in pieces the iron, the bronze, the clay, the silver, and the gold—the great God has made known to the king what will come to pass after this. The dream is certain, and its interpretation is sure.

Verses 31–45

If we look closely at this dream and the circumstances surrounding it, we can see that some urgent matters were unfolding. The king was disturbed by this dream because of its intensity and his nagging remembrance of the details. He knew it contained an important message, but he could not make sense of it. All of this kept him up at night, which made him unbearably cranky from lack of sleep. He did not even think twice about killing his wise men. But there was one man in the kingdom who could make sense of the dream—Daniel, because he was a man in direct relationship with the Dream Giver Himself.

With the help of God, the Giver of dreams, Daniel was able to come before the king and put his mind at ease. Nebuchadnezzar immediately knew that Daniel's interpretation was accurate—it resonated within him. (As I said earlier, people know when their dreams are being accurately interpreted because the meaning resonates within them and brings peace.) The king responded by falling prostrate before Daniel, honoring him and saying, "Truly your God is the God of gods, the Lord of kings, and a revealer of secrets, since you could reveal this secret" (Daniel 2:47). Then the king rewarded Daniel, gave him many great gifts, and promoted him to rule over the whole province of Babylon and be the chief administrator over all the country's wise men.

Interestingly, many historians conclude that Nebuchadnezzar's dream foretold the rise and fall of the Babylonians, the Medo-Persians, the Greeks and the Romans. God revealed the future to a world ruler. Why does He do that kind of thing through dreams? He obviously wants to communicate with us about our lives and our futures!

The Humbling of a King

The Bible records another dream King Nebuchadnezzar had while resting one day in his palace. The dream troubled him so much that he called for the wise men of Babylon to interpret the dream, but they could not tell him what the dream meant. Lastly, Daniel, chief of the wise men showed up, and Nebuchadnezzar shared his dream with Daniel in his own words:

> I was looking, and behold,
> A tree in the midst of the earth,
> And its height was great.
> The tree grew and became strong;
> Its height reached to the heavens,
> And it could be seen to the ends of all the earth.
> Its leaves were lovely,
> Its fruit abundant,
> And in it was food for all.
> The beasts of the field found shade under it,
> The birds of the heavens dwelt in its branches,
> And all flesh was fed from it.
>
> Daniel 4:10–12

The king's dream painted a lovely picture up to that point, and then something changed in it. He told Daniel that a watcher, a holy one, came down from heaven and cried out in the dream,

> Chop down the tree and cut off its branches,
> Strip off its leaves and scatter its fruit.
> Let the beasts get out from under it,
> And the birds from its branches.
> Nevertheless leave the stump and roots in the earth,
> Bound with a band of iron and bronze,
> In the tender grass of the field.
> Let it be wet with the dew of heaven,
> And let him graze with the beasts

On the grass of the earth.
Let his heart be changed from that of a man,
Let him be given the heart of a beast,
And let seven times pass over him.

This decision is by the decree of the watchers,
And the sentence by the word of the holy ones,
In order that the living may know
That the Most High rules in the kingdom of men,
Gives it to whomever He will,
And sets over it the lowest of men.

Verses 14–17

Nebuchadnezzar then asked Daniel to declare the interpretation of the dream since none of the other wise men could do so and since "the Spirit of the Holy God" was in him (verse 18).

The dream astonished Daniel. The first thing he declared was that he would much rather wish this dream on the king's enemies rather than on the king himself. (Not every dream has a rosy meaning, as this one certainly shows, but the message is always worth searching out.) Daniel then relayed the dream's shocking message to the king:

The tree that you saw, which grew and became strong . . . it is you, O king, who have grown and become strong; for your greatness has grown and reaches to the heavens, and your dominion to the end of the earth.

And inasmuch as the king saw a watcher, a holy one, coming down from heaven and saying, "Chop down the tree and destroy it . . ."; this is the interpretation . . . : They shall drive you from men, your dwelling shall be with the beasts of the field, and they shall make you eat grass like oxen. They shall wet you with the dew of heaven, and seven times shall pass over you, till you know that the Most High rules in the kingdom of men, and gives it to whomever He chooses.

And inasmuch as they gave the command to leave the stump and roots of the tree, your kingdom shall be assured to you, after you come to know that Heaven rules. Therefore, O king, let my advice be acceptable to you; break off your sins by being righteous, and your iniquities by showing mercy to the poor. Perhaps there may be a lengthening of your prosperity.

Verses 20, 22–27

The Bible records that about a year later, Nebuchadnezzar was walking through his palace and said to himself, "Is not this great Babylon, that I have built for a royal dwelling by my mighty power and for the honor of my majesty?" (verse 30). At the moment, a voice came from heaven and said:

King Nebuchadnezzar, to you it is spoken: the kingdom has departed from you! And they shall drive you from men, and your dwelling shall be with the beasts of the field. They shall make you eat grass like oxen; and seven times shall pass over you, until you know that the Most High rules in the kingdom of men, and gives it to whomever He chooses.

Verses 31–32

And that is exactly what happened. History records that Nebuchadnezzar lived in the field like an animal for seven years. He ate grass like an ox, his hair grew like eagles' feathers and his nails grew like claws. (He must have been quite a sight!) After seven years, he was restored:

And at the end of the time I, Nebuchadnezzar, lifted my eyes to heaven, and my understanding returned to me; and I blessed the Most High and praised and honored Him who lives forever . . .

At the same time my reason returned to me, and for the glory of my kingdom, my honor and splendor returned to me. My counselors and nobles resorted to me, I was restored to my kingdom, and excellent majesty was added to me. Now I, Nebuchadnezzar, praise and extol and honor the King of heaven, all of whose works

125

WHAT YOUR DREAMS ARE TELLING YOU

are truth, and His ways justice. And those who walk in pride He is able to put down.

Verses 34, 36–37

This dream story again shows how remarkable it is that God chose to give dreams to a ruler who seemingly led only for his own benefit and glory. Yet the dreams sent to this king were not wasted or ignored. On two occasions Nebuchadnezzar honored the correct interpretation of a dream, acknowledged God as the Giver of the dream and rewarded the dream interpreter.

The Nativity Dreams

Behind the scenes of the Nativity story in the Bible are five dreams. God could have used any method to communicate with Joseph or the Magi who came looking for a king, but He used *dreams*. This story shows us how much God values this communication portal. If God values dreams so much that He would choose to communicate through them at such a time of monumental historical importance as the Nativity, then we should value dreams, too.

Dream 1: Take Mary as Your Wife

The Bible records that Joseph was taken aback when he learned of his fiancée Mary's pregnant state (and understandably so). It took a dream from God to convince him that this was the moment all Israel had been waiting for:

> Then Joseph her husband, being a just man, and not wanting to make her a public example, was minded to put her away secretly. But while he thought about these things, behold, an angel of the Lord appeared to him in a dream, saying, "Joseph, son of David, do not be afraid to take to you Mary your wife, for that which is conceived in her is of the Holy Spirit. And she will bring forth a Son, and you shall call His name JESUS, for He will save His people from their sins."

So all this was done that it might be fulfilled which was spoken by the Lord through the prophet, saying: "Behold, the virgin shall be with child, and bear a Son, and they shall call His name Immanuel," which is translated, "God with us."

Then Joseph, being aroused from sleep, did as the angel of the Lord commanded him and took to him his wife, and did not know her till she had brought forth her firstborn Son. And he called His name JESUS.

Matthew 1:19–25

I have read the phrase "Joseph . . . being a just man" many times. But one day as I was rereading this story, I happened to see it this way: "Joseph, being *just a man*," and I thought to myself, *Well, Joseph was indeed a* just *man, but he was also* just a man *and was about to face situations that would go far beyond a man's natural wisdom and abilities.*

Think about it. Joseph is committed to marry someone he loves—someone he trusts—and she says she is pregnant? By the Holy Spirit? This seemed as crazy as Noah building an ark for an earth that had never seen rain. Joseph wrestled with this news in his mind. While he was sleeping—in a place of rest, where he was not struggling to figure out this mystery—God spoke to him, using a dream. God could have used any method to communicate this vital message, but He chose a dream.

Peace or rest provides a place for truth to grow. When you are at rest, you are not anxious or uptight about anything. Many people are presently going through difficult times of great uncertainty that beg for hope, direction and wisdom. Many do not know what to do. In the midst of crisis, God is sending dreams. The Jewish prophet Joel foretold that there would be days when dreams would be common (see Joel 2:28).

I find that people are remembering more of their dreams and that those dreams are having more of an impact. We can use dreams to our advantage and gain direction and understanding when our waking hours are troubling us. People try to figure out their problems with their own natural minds during the daytime hours—what to do, when to do it, how to do it. But when we are sleeping and at rest, not struggling to get an answer, God can deposit the answer. We do not argue in a dream or reason it away. It just is what it is. I understand lucid dreaming (being aware that you are dreaming while it is happening), but there are some dreams that we cannot change no matter what, and those dreams are the most important to pay attention to.

Joseph definitely was not going to get his answer from reading a book by someone else who had experienced the same thing before. Such a thing had never happened. And Joseph knew that if he did not gain some understanding and do something, the religious leaders would find out about Mary's condition and there would be serious trouble. So God sent a dream, and Joseph listened and did exactly as he was told.

Dream 2: The Wise Men's Dream

Some time after Jesus was born, Magi or wise men from the East showed up in Jerusalem. Looking for the prophesied Messiah, they hoped to honor Him with some extravagant gifts. They inquired of King Herod about the child, and the Bible says,

> When Herod the king heard this, he was troubled, and all Jerusalem with him. . . .
> Then Herod, when he had secretly called the wise men, determined from them what time the star appeared. And he sent them to Bethlehem and said, "Go and search carefully for the young Child, and when you have found Him, bring back word to me, that I may come and worship Him also."
> When they heard the king, they departed; and behold, the star which they had seen in the East went before them, till it came and stood over where the young Child was. When they saw the star, they rejoiced with exceedingly great joy. And when they had come into

the house, they saw the young Child with Mary His mother, and fell down and worshiped Him. And when they had opened their treasures, they presented gifts to Him: gold, frankincense, and myrrh.

Matthew 2:3, 7–11

Everyone was happy. The wise men had found Jesus. Jesus and His family received some pretty awesome gifts. And now the wise men were about to follow Herod's instructions and return to tell him where Jesus was. They had no reason to suspect anything. Herod had said he wanted to worship Jesus also. But even if they had been unsure about Herod's motives, they were unlikely to go against a "request" from the king of the land, who could hunt them down and kill them if they chose to ignore it.

As the Magi were getting ready to leave, however, they all had the same dream. And consider this—children's Bible stories usually depict three wise men, but most likely there were more than three. It is incredible when two people have the same dream, let alone three or more! But because the message was so important, God gave them all the same dream. If they all had not dreamed the same thing, they probably would not have gone against Herod's instructions.

The Bible says, "Then, being divinely warned in a dream that they should not return to Herod, they departed for their own country another way" (verse 12). Had they not heeded the message of the dream they shared, Herod would have killed Jesus. This dream revealed the secrets of Herod's heart, shown later when Herod ordered that all the boys under two years old in and around Bethlehem be murdered.

God will often confirm His Word with more than one person. Can you imagine if just one of the wise men had had the dream? The others would have responded, "Big deal that you had a dream! We're not going to put our lives on the line with Herod because of *your* dream. We didn't have that dream—you had it. This isn't about us; it's about you." But things did not happen that way. God confirmed His Word with each of the Magi. When something is really important, God has and will give more than one person the same dream.

Dream 3: Leave Now!

Just after the wise men left, Joseph had his second recorded dream. The Bible tells it this way:

> Now when they had departed, behold, an angel of the Lord appeared to Joseph in a dream, saying, "Arise, take the young Child and His mother, flee to Egypt, and stay there until I bring you word; for Herod will seek the young Child to destroy Him."
>
> When he arose, he took the young Child and His mother by night and departed for Egypt, and was there until the death of Herod, that it might be fulfilled which was spoken by the Lord through the prophet, saying, "Out of Egypt I called My Son."
>
> Matthew 2:13–15

Acting quickly on the very clear message in this dream not only saved the lives of Joseph and his family; it also fulfilled a seven-hundred-year-old prophecy given by the Hebrew prophet Hosea.

Dreams 4 and 5: Return and Live Here

The Bible records two more dreams that God gave to Joseph to get him and his family to the right place:

> Now when Herod was dead, behold, an angel of the Lord appeared in a dream to Joseph in Egypt, saying, "Arise, take the young Child and His mother, and go to the land of Israel, for those who sought the young Child's life are dead." Then he arose, took the young Child and His mother, and came into the land of Israel.
>
> But when he heard that Archelaus was reigning over Judea instead of his father Herod, he was afraid to go there. And being warned by God in a dream, he turned aside into the region of Galilee. And he

came and dwelt in a city called Nazareth, that it might be fulfilled which was spoken by the prophets, "He shall be called a Nazarene."

Matthew 2:19–23

The Christmas story tends to revolve around a woman and a baby in a manger, but behind the scenes was a man who was dreaming and a group of men who all had the same dream on the same night—an amazing occurrence. These dreams saved lives and brought direction at just the right time. In two cases, these dreams also led to the fulfilling of prophecy spoken hundreds of years before.

When God gave a dream, these people wisely listened and responded.

God Gives Dreams and Interpretations

Bible stories from thousands of years ago can seem somewhat disconnected from our lives today. But you and I walk through difficult circumstances in uncertain times, just as Joseph, Nebuchadnezzar, Daniel and Jesus' family did. If you try to get your mind around your problems in the daytime, your mind can play tricks on you. It can accuse you of being irrational, being fearful or not giving credence to information that may be coming from God.

What does God do to help? He speaks to you in your dreams, when you are at rest. Since God gives dreams, He is always the best source to consult when trying to understand your current dreams or reinterpret those dreams you had in the past.

For your sake and for the sake of others, pay attention to your dreams. Dreams from the Dream Giver, the voice of Truth, may lead you to safety and prevent you from being in the wrong place at the wrong time. The historical record of the Bible is full of events in which God-given dreams did just that.

TAKEAWAYS

- God gives dreams and their interpretations. He is always the best source to consult.
- God sends dreams to everyone. Even the mostly unlikely people are receiving dreams that can change the course of history.
- Do your part to listen to the dreams you receive and act on them—for your sake and for the sake of others.

9

HOW TO REAWAKEN YOUR DREAMS

Situation: I had an unknown growth and pain in my pelvic area.

Dream: I went to see my midwife, and she told me I needed a specific kind of oil.

Solution: I woke up and knew this was my answer. I bought the oil capsules, and the growth and pain went away and did not come back.

We can often achieve our life dreams or ambitions with the aid of the dreams we have at night. There are dreams we reach for and dreams that reach for us. We all have ambitions in life—those things we set our courses to achieve. These life dreams of what we want to accomplish are the ones we can control. However, the dreams that reach for us while we sleep can and often will play a big part in helping us achieve our life dreams.

In 1986 a group of eight adults in their twenties had a vision to build a mission center in a neighboring country. At that time the government did not look favorably on foreign workers doing "missionary" work, even though the mission would have a school that would better educate the children in the area. It would take a miracle to obtain permanent visas to stay in the country longer than ninety days at a time.

Their miracle was set in motion by a dream. A few nights before heading to the government office to request permanent visas for his team, Ben, the leader of the group, dreamed that he had to go through seven doors, and upon going through the final door he stepped into a bright, shining light.

When he arrived at the consulate, Ben was directed to one person after another until he finally arrived at the office of the man whose signature was required on every visa—the seventh person or door he had to pass through. Ben sat outside his office for three hours until being called in for an interview to discuss the visa request.

When Ben walked through the door of the official's office, he stepped into the bright light of the sun coming through a large picture window. The official expressed reluctance to give the group permanent visas (Ben had been told to expect, at best, a one-year visa), but the next day he signed the papers granting each team member a permanent visa. Twenty-seven years later, this mission has taught thousands of students and is a respected pillar in the community. Ben's night dream foretold of the perseverance required so they could work in the country and accomplish the team's vision.

Life can also deal out some bitter blows that can flatten our life dreams. Has that happened to you? There is a syndrome present in many cultures around the world where the one who rises above the rest is the one who gets cut down. Maybe this has happened to you. Have you ever started to step out and shine in a particular area, only to be criticized, told you are showing off or accused of having ulterior motives? A thick skin and a load of perseverance are valuable assets for anyone who wants to succeed at anything these days.

Opposition always arises for those who have a life dream. It can come in the form of distractions, busyness, the negative opinion of others or a misguided personal belief system. Some opposition is so painful that people shut down any attempt to achieve their dreams. Many people get caught up in this kind of mess and then jump through all kinds of hoops, trying to find the truth they need to guide their lives. All along, however, the truth is being communicated to them in their dreams, as they sleep.

The answers are there for the desperate. Guidance is available for those who are losing their life dreams—and even losing their lives—because of lack of vision. It is available for those who have made wrong choices, gotten into difficult marriages, wound up in bad jobs or who just do not know what to do. No matter your past, you have a chance to dream again and really live as you were created to live.

Remember the dream in chapter 7 about the woman who found the baby in a garbage bag in a parking garage, only to discover that *she* was actually the "baby"? Remember how the dream showed that she was rescuing the baby—herself—by taking back control from those who had thrown the child away, along with all of its potential? This is a perfect example of how a night dream can direct us to move forward in life with confidence to find our destiny.

Let's look at dreams you have had in the past and how you can awaken them once again so they can bring you hope, encouragement and power for your present and into your future. I am talking here about reawakening our night dreams, but often night dreams are a picture of our life dreams and ambitions. When you reawaken or remember your night dreams of old and reconnect with them, it can allow what once excited you—your passions, the things that made you "fly"—to come to life again. Reawakening night dreams can help reawaken life dreams.

Earlier, I asked you to think about a dream that you have had that falls into one of these three categories:

- The same dream recurring more than once
- Different dreams that have a similar theme
- Dreams that are so vivid, you feel as if you were there

I want you to do the same thing again, but this time I want to lead you through three steps to reawaken your dreams. They are *remember*, *reawaken your heart* and *respond*. We will take these steps one at a time, together, and see where we end up. It will be in a good place!

Step 1: Remember

From birth, everyone has something they have been wired for or designed to do. Dreams remind and reawaken us. Let's go back to your starting place. Did something take you off course? What got you moving in a direction that was not designed for you? It is never too late to get back on track.

For this *remember* step, go to the dream journal at the back of this book and take a few minutes to record your responses to these questions:

- Write down a dream you had while growing up. What was the main content of that dream? (If you had nightmares, do not focus on those right now. Just think about the dreams you would look forward to having at night. My favorite dream was swimming underwater for long distances without coming up for air. I could go really fast! I also had many dreams about standing in front of people and having a message to deliver, even though I was not dressed for the part—I was in my pajamas.)
- What were you the most excited about after having the dream?

136

- What was going on in your life at the time of the dream?
- When did the dream stop?
- How does this dream connect to what is happening in your life right now?
- What would it take to turn this dream into something extraordinary for you as an adult?

For nightmares or dreams that left you with a negative feeling, ask yourself the same questions as above, and also this question:

- Was there something that this dream was trying to shut down in your life? (In chapter 6 I talked about how to "flip" your dreams. The very area where you are attacked is often the area where you are supposed to excel. What the enemy was trying to shut down through a lying dream, you can now see come to life!)

A Little More about Nightmares

Nightmares are usually not something anyone wants to remember. Someone told me the following nightmare and asked me to interpret it. This dreamer shared that some of her present dreams are so terrifying and real that it is hard to sleep. Her life has been going well lately, and she does not understand why she is having these dreams now since the events in them seem related to things that happened many years ago. Note that the person called this dream mild in comparison to others she has been having:

I am in a house. No doors except for ones that lead to the outside. There is a long library bookshelf with books and toys, and some empty shelves are between me and the main front door. I am on a round rug. The toilet is behind me. No door. Next to that is a room labeled "rape room." People come and go, but they do not look at each other. Heads down. I hear screams from the room. A man comes and grabs me, takes me into the rape room and rapes me. A long line of men stands behind him. I get up to go to the bathroom in between men. A lady grabs me. Tells me to go to the helicopter pad outside on the lawn. She wants me to be safe. The guy hears her and beats her. I create a distraction. She goes around the bookshelves and out the front door. The guy takes me and burns my back. I don't cry. I see outside that the helicopter is leaving. I am too weak to run. A car crashes into the rape room. I watch men fight over the damage. Then I wake up.

This dream is showing that this woman feels trapped by things that took place in her past. There are no doors or ways of escape except the one door that leads her outside, which represents freedom. There is only *one* way out. She has to face her fears to be truly free. She is also aware of others in the same situation. That they had their heads down and avoided looking at each other speaks of shame, fear and total slavery to the sexual and physical abuse going on. She will have to be determined to get free, but freedom is coming for sure.

Toilets represent places of personal cleansing where waste is gotten rid of, and places where things can be "flushed." God provided a way of escape (a helicopter) for this dreamer, but she missed it since she was too weak to run or fight. It may be a battle for her to get out of this situation, but the sting is from her past because it "burned her back." A car crashes right into the rape room, providing another way of escape, and it causes a distraction so she can get set free.

I believe this dream is also showing this woman that she can provide an answer to victims of abuse—to those who are enslaved to broken people who have no regard for anything but their own self-gratification. This could very well be a calling dream for this person, calling her to become a help to those who are caught in such situations. The library shelves in the dream might contain information she could use to educate herself about this, or possibly books written on circumstances such as these. Getting more information would help bring her and others back to a very innocent time in their lives (represented by toys on the shelves).

I received a follow-up email from this dreamer saying that my interpretation of her dream was accurate and meaningful to her. Remembering is a powerful tool. We are to remember the good, but sometimes we also have to remember the bad so that we can forgive, get healed and move on. I honestly think the dreams this woman is having in the present are bringing to the surface unresolved issues so that she can get free of them. It is kind of like what boiling a liquid does; it brings the impurities to the surface so you can get rid of them and be left with what is pure. This dream also gives hope to the dreamer that not only is God providing a way of escape for her so that she can be free; but that she will also be able to help others experience the same freedom. This and the other nightmares she is having right now could leave her completely discouraged, but if she flips them to see the light in the midst of the darkness, she can be whole, and in time, she can comfort others with the same comfort she received.

Sometimes people do not want to remember their past or face their nightmares because of what is there. But if you are receiving "bad" dreams that you do not understand, it is important to deal with them so that what needs to be put to rest can rest, and what needs to come alive for the future can come alive.

Step 2: Reawaken Your Heart

Sometimes we shut down parts of our hearts during a crisis or in response to pain, just so we can cope and survive. This is not a good long-term strategy for happiness and success. Have you shut down any part of your heart? To begin the process of reawakening your heart, I recommend doing the following:

Let Yourself Dream Again

Two realities exist—one based on Truth and one based on Lie— and both are extremely real. It is like the movie *The Matrix*, in which the reality most people perceive is a simulated counterfeit of the real world. We live in the world as we perceive it, and our perceptions begin to define our opinions, our worldview and how we see ourselves. Counterfeit perceptions from the Lie source are just as real to us as those from the Truth source. Truth is always stronger if we will let it into our lives, though.

What God extends to you in dreams is truth—truth about yourself, truth about your world, truth about God Himself. You will experience freedom to the degree that you align yourself with the truth. It is hard to believe that you can do the impossible or change history in and of yourself. But when you see yourself the way God sees you, that point of view will reawaken your dreams and keep you in forward motion that will connect you with your destiny.

You are given night dreams for a reason, so shutting them down or doing nothing to remember them when you wake up robs you of information and experiences you were meant to have. Remembering your past dreams will help reawaken your heart, but you also have to give yourself permission to remember and pursue your dreams again. Maybe you just need to believe that the dreams you have at night, which often reflect or serve as an inspiration for life dreams, are legitimate. They are, and you do not need anyone's approval to dream or to walk out your dreams. Approval from the Spirit of Truth who gives dreams is all the approval you need.

You cannot always control what comes at you from the outside to hinder your dreams. But you can do something about what you believe on the inside. If you have shut down your dreams in any way, give yourself permission to dream again. This can be as simple as saying to yourself and to God, "I want to dream again."

Forgive, Let Go and Heal

Someone told me about a dream they had of walking into a clinic and seeing a female doctor and three middle-aged women. The women were fully clothed, but had IV poles going up their skirts into their reproductive areas so that the doctor could give them medicine that would heal their barrenness. One proverb says, "Hope deferred makes the heart sick, but when the desire comes, it is a tree of life" (Proverbs 13:12). Both this proverb and the dream are saying that we need to receive healing so that we can "conceive" or "birth" new life and be fruitful. None of us is exempt from the battlefield. Each of us battles daily for our well-being, for our quality of life, for meaning and purpose and ultimately to know our Creator. After a prolonged season of pain or hardship, healing is needed.

Maybe you have heard the statement "Hurting people hurt people." When people hurt each other, the pain is often excruciating and can act like a bridge that blows up in the middle of our life path, creating a massive hindrance against us advancing into a good future. If this has happened to you (and it probably has, or will in the future), you have to make a decision to forgive and move on. You cannot allow your past to dictate your future. The past is over and cannot be changed, but the future is in front of you, with vast open fields of opportunity and accomplishments that await you.

Let's face it. You can either be pitiful or powerful, but you cannot be both. If you continue to agree with hurt, anger and bitterness in response to life's blows, you will empower them and sabotage your future. But if you agree with forgiveness, freedom and success, you will empower those strengths and go on to achieve seemingly unreachable goals for yourself.

Healing will come as you forgive and let go of the residue of hurt—bitterness, anger, resentment, grief and the like. Whether or not you are ever able to restore what has been lost, forgive and let go for *your* sake, so that you can have a whole heart and so that nothing can hold you back from your dreams.

Take a few minutes to tell God, "I turn over these hurts to You [be specific about them]. I ask that You make these things right. I am choosing to forgive and let go of these hurts I've experienced. Heal my heart and awaken it again to the dreams that You give to me."

Stay Encouraged—You Are Not Alone

Life tries us and can be wearisome. Most of us want to escape the wearisome part of the process. It is demanding, and it is demanding for a reason. Perhaps more than any other people group, the Jewish people have experienced prolonged seasons of persecution from all sides. During a critical time in their history, the writer of the book of Hebrews said to them, "And we desire that each one of you show the same diligence to the full assurance of hope until the end, that you do not become sluggish, but imitate those who through faith and patience inherit the promises" (Hebrews 6:11–12).

The success stories of people who overcame great obstacles to obtain great victories are endless. Dreams from God are promises and invite us to partner with Him. In the same book of Hebrews, the writer records an awe-inspiring list of people who, throughout Jewish history, persevered and maintained their faith even when their lives were seemingly headed in the opposite direction from what God had promised (see Hebrews chapter 11).

The ways available to us to overcome our challenges are often narrow and restricted by pressures around us. But narrow pathways cause us to drop the baggage we do not need in the places we are headed. As you are going through life, do not become discouraged or consider it strange when you face difficulty. It is important to understand that the process of life is demanding. That is part of the journey.

The writer of Hebrews gave one more piece of advice that I find essential to staying the course. He told us to think about how we can inspire "love and good deeds" from each other, and he said that we should gather together often, "encouraging one another" along the way (Hebrews 10:24–25 NIV). If you and I are going to reach our destinies, we need others alongside us who will remind us of the future and hope that is set before us.

We need to remind other people of the same thing, too, especially since so much that stands in opposition to the truth comes at all of us. We must come alongside each other and continually call each other to a reality of the truth about ourselves, our connection to God and God's future for all of us.

Step 3: Respond

You can do a few practical things to reawaken your dreams. Let's look at some responses that will help you dream again.

Make Your Dreams a Priority

The Raramuri people of Northern Mexico set up their sleeping arrangements so that they could wake during the night to discuss their dreams with one another. They also make dreams a frequent part of their morning conversations.[1] I am not suggesting that you need to change your bedroom around, but here are a few things you can do to make your dreams a priority:

- Before you go to bed, ask the Spirit of Truth to guide you into truth through a dream. As the saying goes, "Ask and you shall receive." And if you do not receive right away, keep on asking!

- Try to wake up to soft music or wake up naturally on days when you do not have to get up at a specific time. When you wake up, lie in bed peacefully for a minute or two without starting to think about the day. I mentioned in the first chapter that typically within five minutes of waking up, you have forgotten half of your dream. Within ten minutes, 90 percent is gone. Taking a few moments of reflection after a night's sleep will go a long way toward helping you remember your dreams.

- Keep a dream journal or notebook next to your bed (following the format of the journal at the back of this book). If you wake up in the middle of the night and remember a dream you just

143

had, write it down. When you wake up in the morning, write down any dreams you remember. If you are in the shower, getting ready for your day, and you remember a dream, write it down. The key is to capture the moment when you remember your dreams and write those dreams down as soon as you can.

- Talk about your dreams with someone you trust. If you're married, have children or have a roommate, in the morning ask, "Do you remember any of your dreams from last night?" Don't ask, "Did you have any dreams last night?" because everyone dreams every night. The real question is whether they remember them. Often the meaning of your dream will come to light as you talk about it with someone. You may also find that the other person can help you understand your dream language to see more clearly what your dream is telling you.

Listen to the Message

I have included a sample of an excellent dream journal format in this book so that you can get into the habit of writing down your dreams, processing them and getting something out of them. They say it takes 21 days to build a new habit. Take the next 21 days (and then beyond) to build the habit of writing down and processing the dreams you remember when you wake up.

By asking yourself the questions from the dream journal at the back, you will start to connect the dots. You will begin to understand your dream language more clearly so that you can take appropriate action in response. Remember that the message you receive in a dream is *your* message, not mine. It is *your* opportunity, not someone else's. Make the most of it!

It goes without saying that God is smart. He is so wise that He will use foolish things to perplex self-proclaimed wise people. Recently I did a television interview on a major news station where the reporter did not believe dreams were real or were for today. I felt sorry for her. Here she dreamed every night—as did every viewer watching—yet she discounted the reality and importance of the messages all of us receive during our sleeping hours through our dreams.

This reporter framed the interview we did in such a way that the idea of dreams and the messages they contain looked foolish and insignificant. After it was over, the comments people left on the station's website varied—everything came in from agreeing with the interviewer completely to standing in total opposition to her viewpoint. I was amazed to see how this slanted interview caused such a stir in people's hearts.

On a recent radio interview call-in program, the phone lines lit up and emails came pouring in as we asked listeners to give us their dreams for interpretation. I was sitting next to the computer screen in the studio, and I watched as the emails scrolled down the page. The announcer had to make the statement on the air that "there is no way we can possibly answer all of these emails." That interview showed how very hungry people are to know what messages are being spoken to them while they sleep.

It is hard to listen to something you do not believe in. If you are like that reporter, still uncertain about all that I have been saying about the importance of dreams and their messages for us, remember that the scientifically proven facts are in: You dream . . . every night. Thousands of years of history show the extraordinary impact dreams have had on our world. Believe and listen. You will be glad you did.

Also, keep your listening antennae up. It is easy to become too familiar with your dreams. Have you ever woken up and thought, *That was a cool dream*, or *That was weird*, but then you did not bother to write down the dream or think about it again? Some people would give just about anything to receive wise advice about a business proposal, a relationship or a direction in life, yet they do not realize they are getting advice in their dreams! You are getting this same advice, so tune in and listen—really listen. And then listen some more.

Do Something with the Message

While not every dream requires immediate action and some require no action at all, it is good to keep a record of your dreams anyway. Just because a dream does not make sense to you when you have it does not mean that it will not make sense at some point in the future. If you can learn to value dreams as a valid communication method, you will begin to receive more information from them. The first practical thing you can do is write them down.

Throughout this book, I have given a number of recommendations about what to do with certain dreams. For example, if you have a dream about your teeth falling out, get the facts about a situation you are facing and take a deeper look before acting. If you have a falling dream, consider whether you are feeling the need to be in control all of the time. Consider that maybe the chaos you are experiencing is bringing about positive change for a new kind of order in your life, or maybe your dream is telling you that you need to take some strategic action to set things in order.

Be cautious that you do not act impulsively on information you may receive in a dream, though, especially if you dream something bad about another person. Many relationships have been compromised or have even been put to an end because of this. Just write that kind of dream down, and over the next weeks and months, see what happens. Some dreams come to a person simply for contemplation or prayer—not for any other reason. You should use this practice of moving forward with caution for dreams about catastrophic events, as well. Messages in dreams can be the vehicle, but it is important to use wisdom as you consider what action to take in response.

Regardless of your dream, use it for your good. Explore the possibilities and make the most of the information you have been given.

Go to the Spirit of Truth

In chapter 3 I gave you seven guiding principles for interpretation. The last one was to connect the dream with the Giver of dreams. We have learned that dreams can come from three sources: Self, Lie and Truth. While it is good to know yourself, getting more full of yourself certainly is not helpful. And connecting with lies is not on the list of the best practices for a happy life, either. Connecting with Truth, however—the Spirit of Truth, God Himself, your Creator—is the best thing you could ever do to reawaken lost dreams—and to reawaken *life* dreams.

If a dream is truly given to you from God, you can begin to connect with God and find out your true purpose and destiny in life. We all have questions deep down in our hearts like, *Why am I here? What am I made for? Why was I made this way? How can I connect with my real purpose in life?* These questions and others like them are honest questions that deserve answers. Connecting with the Giver of life, the One who made you, will cause the lights to go on in your heart, and your life will begin to make sense.

Dreams can speak right to your spirit and cause you to awaken spiritually. When you begin to experience healing on any level, you start to live again. God is the Author of life, and He is actively trying to communicate with us. He gives dreams because He has given you a life to live and wants to help you live it to the full.

Do not let religion bog down your thinking about what God is like. God is way too big to fit into your mind, and He is much better and much different than you presently think. God, the Giver of dreams, will do exceedingly, abundantly above all that you could ask or imagine (see Ephesians 3:20). I think that is awesome. It is time to reawaken your dreams and to dream again!

TAKEAWAYS

- Let yourself dream again. Remember the dreams you receive at night and allow them to inspire you and energize your vision for your life dreams during the day. You are given dreams for a reason. Receive the information and experiences that you were meant to have.

- Do not sabotage your future with bitterness, anger or unforgiveness. Forgive, and let go of past injustices for *your* sake, so that you can have a whole heart and so that nothing can hold you back from your dreams.

- Make your dreams a priority. Listen to them, and do something with the messages you receive.

10

DREAM ON AND LIVE

Situation: A lace sweater pattern was incorrectly written for row 7 of a 24-row pattern repeat. I spent a lot of time trying to figure it out but was ready to give up on making the sweater.

Dream: I saw the correct pattern instructions for row 7.

Solution: Upon waking, I wrote down the pattern, tried knitting it and it worked. I was able to let the pattern company know what was wrong so that they could correct the pattern.

It is June 6, 2002, in Salt Lake City, Utah. Posters are hung all over town that picture the face of a sweet fourteen-year-old girl who was kidnapped out of her bedroom the previous night. Search teams assemble and begin to scour the mountainsides, hills and streams, looking frantically for this young girl who two days earlier received awards for her academics and physical fitness from her intermediate school. Elizabeth Smart, an up-and-coming harpist, is missing. Shocked friends and family are frantic in their efforts to bring her back.

The posters promising reward money are displayed everywhere as the search continues for Elizabeth. Her father, Ed Smart, is released from the hospital on June 6, after collapsing from exhaustion. The search for the girl continues for weeks and months, with countless TV interviews and pleas with the kidnapper to bring her back home safely.

A couple of months after the kidnapping, on August 28, Sean Hannity interviews Ed Smart on Fox News. Smart tells Hannity that he has had a dream about Elizabeth. In his dream, she came walking through the door and gave him a hug. He says that holding her tightly in the dream, he was encouraged that she is still alive, and he awoke just knowing that she is out there somewhere.

On March 12, 2003, after nine months of anguish for the Smart family, Elizabeth Smart is rescued from her abuser and is safely returned home. But just two months after the kidnapping, Mr. Smart had a dream—a dream that gave him hope until his daughter was found.

I wrote this book because I meet scores of people who have no hope and do not know what to do. Some are at the point of taking their lives or ending their marriage, while others are very successful in life by the world's standards but are unhappy with the results of their success. As Elizabeth Smart and her family know, life deals many a tough hand. It is easy to turn away from the path we have been designed to walk. Dreams are a way to introduce truth that helps people get back on track after all the things that have happened to them in the past. No matter who you are or what has happened to you, the keys I have shared in these pages will help unlock your door of understanding into messages and solutions that are coming to you from your dreams.

As you read through and process this final chapter, I want you to know that there is one main message you must hear: *Dream on!*

See old dreams come to life again. See new dreams bring new life for now and for the future. Do not give up on your journey. You are the only one who can live your life.

This Is It

You only have one shot at life. What are you going to do with it? The world was stunned when Michael Jackson died suddenly in June 2009, just as he was preparing a series of comeback concerts titled "This Is It." Sadly for Michael, that was it.

Consider that this is it for you, too. How are you going to make the most of your life? You can find your course and get out of any rut you are in. Ample help is available for you so that you can truly live, no matter what changes you need to make.

What is holding you back? What are you settling for, and what should you be reaching for? What door has closed that has tempted you to believe there is no other door? Unopened doors are just potential for new things. Are you allowing your past to dictate your future? The sky really is the limit. If you pay attention, your dreams will help take you where you need to be.

Go back in time and try to grasp the fun and exciting dreams you have had. Were you on a horse? Were you flying? Were you singing on a stage? Remembering early childhood dreams can help you regain the innocence you were born with.

God created the portal of dreams. He speaks to you through dreams. God Himself is a dreamer and wants you to have the most incredible life that you possibly can. He is a loving, personal Father-Creator who designed you exactly as He wants you to be. There are no limitations with God, just limitations of your concept of Him and of your own life. You will stay hindered, shortsighted and confined until you connect with God and His purpose for you. You can see only in part, but God has your future clearly in His sight.

Change only comes to those who are responsible to take steps to change. Your past is a setup for a *good* future, not a bad one. Real life comes when your life embodies the truth as you go through pain, frustration and the pressure of daily life. I call this pressure "preparation." In difficulties and hardships, you are prepared for the overcoming, victorious life you were meant to have. Remember that there are endless success stories about people who have overcome insurmountable circumstances to achieve incredible results. The answer is, *Don't quit!* God will make a way when you set your heart and mind to achieve your goals in life.

Farming gives a great picture of how life is. The farmer goes out and works hard to prepare the soil and plant the seed. Then he waits. In time, the ground begins to produce a harvest based on the seeds he planted. Like the farmer, you struggle to plant the seeds of the fruit you want to see in your life. Then you rest, sometimes wondering if your hard work will yield what you are hoping for. And after all that, you experience a breakthrough.

A funny thing to consider is that the farmer achieves the best growth when he adds fertilizer to the soil. I guess that means when you and I are wading through a bunch of manure in life, we can count on a bounty crop!

Sometimes during the long wait before we see signs of the harvest we are hoping for, we get frustrated and want to give up. But then the breakthrough comes, and we enjoy a season of harvest. I have often seen it happen that the moment someone surrenders and lets go—*bam!* Good things happen.

The Power of Encouragement

History has brought us the Age of Enlightenment, the Industrial Age and the Information Age. Now we are in the Connected Age, in which an abundance of advice, instruction and technology is available to make life better for everyone. Search the Internet for an answer to any question you can think of, and you will find something.

Why, then, are so many people having such a hard time in life when we have more information at our fingertips and more ways to get things done than we have ever had before? Maybe it is because what Ecclesiastes 1:18 says in the Bible is true: "In much wisdom there is much grief, and increasing knowledge results in increasing pain" (NASB).

There is a famine in the land today—a famine of encouragement. Encouragement can come through dreams, but it is also supposed to come through *you*! People who impact people are not just information givers. People who impact people are givers of hope and encouragement. Life is deposited into others when you encourage them with the encouragement you have received.

The rewards from helping someone else in a time of need cannot be measured. You and I are designed to help others. People who struggle with depression find that their depression leaves when they serve someone else or get involved with another person's life.

Constant self-focus or "navel-gazing" causes vision to dissipate. When you are constantly looking at yourself, you lose sight of everything and everyone else around you. The way to find rich fulfillment is by helping someone else—a co-worker, a neighbor or someone in a grocery store or a nursing home. When you take a minute to assist a young mother struggling to keep her children from running into the street, it will help you as much as it does her. Nothing lifts your spirit and does your heart more good than doing a good deed when one is needed.

We all need hope. The Jewish prophet Jeremiah said that God has good plans for us: "For I know the thoughts that I think toward you, says the LORD, thoughts of peace and not of evil, to give you a future and a hope" (Jeremiah 29:11). Jesus foretold a day where "because lawlessness [murder, betrayal and deception] will abound, the love of many will grow cold." But He added that the person "who endures to the end shall be saved" (Matthew 24:12–13). During difficult times, we must look up. God wants us to look up. Dreams point us upward and get us through the dismal circumstances we are facing.

At a workshop my husband and I attended, we spent a week focusing on the promises of God found in the Bible. A woman whose daughter had been in a mental hospital brought the girl to the workshop, and we spoke over this young girl the promises of God we had been rehearsing all week long. As a result, the girl was totally healed from depression and from a learning hindrance. How did that happen? Through the power of hope and encouragement.

Most of us are deeply immersed in the reality of bad news. How about some good news? The good news is that God is speaking to you through your dreams, which can transform your life if you listen and respond. When people look into a mirror, what do they usually see? Blemishes—all the stuff they wish was not there. While dreams help us to see the truth, the purpose of dreams is not to point out all that is wrong. They are to help us see who we are from God's point of view and see what we can become. God wants us to look into a different mirror and see His image, because what you focus on is what you will become. If you can see the light God has put inside you, then you will progressively be transformed into that image.

Ultimately, you are the only one who can hold you back. Yet you can conquer a mountain if you take it one step at a time. It is kind of like the video game Pac-Man: Take one bite at a time, and pretty soon you have devoured the whole thing. God will take you as far as you will let Him. So much is ahead of you, if you let God open a path for you. He will make a way where there seems to be no way—if you will look up. In the words of Winston Churchill, "Never, never, never give up."

Be Yourself and Change the World

A few times within these pages, I have asked you to write down some of your dreams using the format of the dream journal at the back of this book. That exercise will help you search out who you are. I have set up the dream journal format so that you can go back over your dreams, categorize them and see how many times you have had a certain dream. Take steps to explore the direction you may be getting from your dreams and see what doors open for you. Search out God, too, and grab hold of why you are here. Do not run away from life—step into it and into the destiny for which you were created.

Respond to your dreams. Be a scientist like Friedrich August von Kekule or Dmitri Mendeleyev and make breakthrough advances in science. Be an inventor like Elias Howe, who developed a machine that revolutionized an industry. Be a doctor like Frederick Banting, and discover a treatment—or better yet, a cure—for a deadly disease. Be like Harriet Tubman and use your dreams to help others find their freedom. Be an author like Robert Louis Stevenson or Mary Shelley and write a book from a dream for others to enjoy for hundreds of years. Be an employee like Julie Gilbert Newrai, Alan Huang, Jeff Johnson or Floyd Ragsdale and solve unsolvable problems at work. Be a singer/songwriter like Paul McCartney and hear melodies in your dreams, then turn them into songs the world sings.

Better yet, just be yourself and change the world because of who you are and the destiny your Creator has given you. Think of yourself as God thinks of you—as an amazing and wonderful creation (see Psalm 139). You are not a mistake. Your life is not a mistake. Your children are not mistakes. Your life will make sense when you connect with the Giver of life—God.

In 1973, I had an encounter with God through Jesus, and Jesus rocked my world. My spiritual hunger caused me to find my purpose and understand *why* I was made and *how* I was made. I considered many choices along my way to finding the "truth" that people like me seem to be searching for. I made a decision that I would only give my life to the One who gave His life for me, and out of all the spiritual teachers and gurus, there was only One who did that—Jesus.

Since that time, my life has been on a pathway of seeking the truth and finding the way. Jesus calls Himself the Way, the Truth and the Life (see John 14:6). He is the way I have found, and I would never, never go back. God does not just have love; God *is* love. And nobody loves me the way He does. It is a win-win going with God through Jesus.

But that is *my* story. If you are searching for answers, too, just ask for them. Say, "God, I have many questions. Show me the Way and the Truth." God really is talking to people. Messages are being sent to you through dreams. These dreams can change your life, and if you will respond to them, you can become an inspiration and a resource to change other people's lives, too.

You have a reason to live. Anything is possible. Inspiration from your dreams is like air in your lungs and strength to run your race. Dream on and live!

TAKEAWAYS

- Surround yourself with sources of encouragement. Dreams point us upward and get us through any difficult circumstances we face. In the words of Winston Churchill, "Never, never, never give up."
- Seek the truth, and you will find it.
- Respond to your dreams and change the world.

DREAM SYMBOLS APPENDIX

Below are some common symbols that appear in dreams. Keep in mind that although these symbols can be helpful, you should never try to interpret your dream by the symbols alone. This appendix should be used only as a supplement to the framework, guidelines and interpretation principles I have included in this book. The dream journal I have also included outlines a fantastic way to process your dreams. Use this appendix in conjunction with the dream journal, and have fun!

Airplanes	Vehicle with groups of people who can see from a higher level
Alligator	Gossip/Big mouth
Altar	Place of surrender or worship
Ant	Industrious/Hard worker
Apples	Fruit or temptation
Arm	Power or strength
Back doors	Doorways to the past
Banks	Stored wealth
Barn	Provision
Basements	Hidden things/Foundations

Bathrooms	Places of cleansing and purifying
Bedrooms	Places of intimacy and rest
Being chased	Past issues trying to attack you or hinder you from advancing
Bicycles	Self-effort
Breast	Nurturing
Bus	Vehicle carrying more than one person
School bus	Training/In school
Camp	Temporary settling or "camping out"
Cave	Hiding place/Protected
Childhood homes	Issues from that time
Clock	Timing
Closet	Stored things/Personal hidden things
Clothing	Coverings
College	Schools of higher learning
Dead relatives	Family issues or themes—good and bad
Dog	Friend or foe (What is the dog doing?)
Door	Openings or closings
Driving your car	Your life
Someone else driving your car	They are in control of your life
Dying	Something ends so something can begin
Earthquake	Sudden release of power—good or bad
Eating bugs	Consuming bad spiritual food
Elementary	Ground level of learning
Elevator	Effortless transport to a new level up or down
Face	Image/Identity
Falling	Life out of control
Farmer	Planting and growing things

158

Forest	Overwhelming situations
Front doors	Future things (Back doors—past things)
Garbage	Neglected areas
Gloves	Covering the work of the hands
Grandmother	Generational influence
Hallways	Transition places
Head	Leadership
Helicopter	Strategic
High school friends	Friends who are in a high level of learning or revisiting that time in life
Hotel	Short stays
Hospital	Place of healing
Kiss	Affection
Living room	Open, receptive place
Lion	Honorable king/Predator
Locked doors	Things not accessible to you
Morning	New day
Motorcycle	Risk-taking spirit
Naked	Transparent
Neck	Directional or strong willed/Turns the vision
Nose	Discernment/Sees real from fake
Parrot	Mocking spirit
Peacock	Show off/Pride/Good display
Pig	Unclean spirit
Pregnant	New birth/Nurturing something new
President	High authority
Rain	Refreshing/Blessing
Running in slow motion	Fear-based/Hindrances
School	Classroom/Training
Shadow	False image

Ships	International transports
Shoes	Cover your walk
Snakes	Lies/Long tales
Spiders	Annoying presence
Stairs	Changing levels up or down/Self-effort
Taking a test	Promotion/Demotion
Teeth falling out	Losing ability to understand
Television	Tell a vision/Something to watch
Tidal wave	Overtaken by something big
Toilet	Personal cleansing
Trains	Movement or training
Tunnel	Hidden passageways
Twister/ Tornado	Personal impact/Rearranging/Stirring things up
Underwater	Seeing things below the surface
Volcano	Explosive/Out of control/Purifying
Weddings	Making commitments
Windows	Limited vision
Winter	A season where things are dormant

DREAM JOURNAL

Build the habit of writing down and searching out your dreams. Here is a good model to follow for documenting your dreams:

Date: Write down the date the dream occurred.

Title: Give your dream a descriptive and memorable title.

Theme: Categorize your dream so that you can see where you have similar patterns, like Flying Dream, Falling Dream, Losing Your Teeth, Naked in Public . . .

Description: Write down a detailed description of your dream.

Summary: Summarize and include the following elements:

1. **Determine the Source:** Truth, Lie, Self or a Mix
2. **Determine the Message:**
   - Are you a participant or an observer?
   - What is the main element or focus of the dream?
   - What is happening in your life right now that may be connected to the dream?
   - Have you had a dream with a similar theme in the past? If yes, what date? What are the differences this time?
   - What is the main message of this dream in a phrase or a short sentence?
3. **Determine your Response:** What action or actions will you take to respond to this dream?

Date: .... **Title:** ....

Theme: ....

Description:

....

....

....

....

....

....

....

....

....

....

....

....

....

....

....

....

....

Summary:

Source: ☐ Truth   ☐ Lie   ☐ Self   ☐ Mix (Check one)

Message:

Are you the ☐ Participant or ☐ Observer?

Main element or focus of the dream?

What is happening in your life right now that may be connected to the dream?

Have you had a dream with a similar theme in the past?
☐ Yes   ☐ No   If yes, what date? _____

What are the differences this time? _____

What is the main message of this dream in a phrase or a short sentence?

Response:

Date: Title:

Theme:

Description:

Summary:

Source: ☐ Truth ☐ Lie ☐ Self ☐ Mix (Check one)

Message:

Are you the ☐ Participant or ☐ Observer?

Main element or focus of the dream?

What is happening in your life right now that may be connected to the dream?

Have you had a dream with a similar theme in the past?
☐ Yes ☐ No If yes, what date? _____

What are the differences this time? _____

What is the main message of this dream in a phrase or a short sentence?

Response:

Date: _____ **Title:** _____

Theme: _____

Description:

_____

_____

_____

_____

_____

_____

_____

_____

_____

_____

_____

_____

_____

_____

_____

_____

Summary:

Source: ☐ Truth ☐ Lie ☐ Self ☐ Mix (Check one)

Message:

Are you the ☐ Participant or ☐ Observer?

Main element or focus of the dream?

_____

What is happening in your life right now that may be connected to the dream?

_____

_____

Have you had a dream with a similar theme in the past?
☐ Yes ☐ No If yes, what date? _____

What are the differences this time? _____

_____

_____

What is the main message of this dream in a phrase or a short sentence?

_____

_____

Response:

_____

_____

_____

Date: .... **Title:** ....

Theme: ....

Description:

_____

_____

_____

_____

_____

_____

_____

_____

_____

_____

_____

_____

_____

_____

_____

_____

_____

_____

Summary:

Source: ☐ Truth ☐ Lie ☐ Self ☐ Mix (Check one)

Message:

Are you the ☐ Participant or ☐ Observer?

Main element or focus of the dream?

_____

What is happening in your life right now that may be connected to the dream?

_____

_____

Have you had a dream with a similar theme in the past?
☐ Yes ☐ No If yes, what date? _____

What are the differences this time? _____

_____

_____

What is the main message of this dream in a phrase or a short
sentence?

_____

_____

Response:

_____

_____

_____

NOTES

Chapter 1: Results When You Listen

1. This section is an adaptation of the content found on Julie's website www.WolfMeansBusiness.com. Used by permission. Co-author David Sluka was part of Julie's team at Best Buy Company, Inc., and experienced firsthand the transformational nature of her work.

2. Faith Hickman Brynie, *Sleep and Dreams: 101 Questions about Sleep and Dreams* (Minneapolis: Twenty-First Century Books, 2006), chapter 2.

3. Derrick Jensen, *Dreams* (New York: Seven Stories Press, 2011), chapter entitled "Other Sides."

4. Brynie, *Sleep and Dreams*, chapter 2.

5. James R. Lewis and Evelyn Dorothy Oliver, *The Dream Encyclopedia*, 2nd ed. (Canton, Mich.: Visible Ink Press, 2009), 64.

6. Dream Moods, "Dream facts and tidbits," Dream Moods, Inc., online, June 5, 2012, http://www.dreammoods.com/dreaminformation/dreamfacts.htm.

7. John N. Oswalt, "Chronology of the Old Testament," *International Standard Bible Encyclopedia*, 1:677; James Orr, M.A., D.D., ed., entry for "Chronology of the Old Testament," *International Standard Bible Encyclopedia*, 1915, http://www.biblestudytools.com/encyclopedias/isbe/chronology-of-the-old-testament.html.

8. Penney Peirce, *Dreams for Dummies®* (Foster City, Calif.: IDG Books Worldwide, 2000), 23.

9. Ibid.

10. Sandra Weintraub, "Cultivate Your Dreams to Find New Solutions," Winston J. Brill & Associates, #179 from R&D Innovator Volume 4, Number 10, October 1995, http://www.winstonbrill.com/bril001/html/article_index/articles151_200.html.

11. O. T. Benfey, "August Kekulé and the Birth of the Structural Theory of Organic Chemistry in 1858," *Journal of Chemical Education*, 35 (1958), 21–23.

12. Kathleen Kiley, "The Role of Dreams," Wellness Insights, LLC, http://kathleenkiley.com/dreams/the-role-of-dreams/; "Frederick Banting," Wikipedia, February 21, 2013, http://en.wikipedia.org/wiki/Frederick_Banting.

13. "Otto Loewi," Wikipedia, March 13, 2013, http://en.wikipedia.org/wiki/Otto_Loewi; D. Todman: "Inspiration from dreams in neuroscience research," *The Internet Journal of Neurology* 9, no. 1 (2008): 10.5580/1b79. See more at http://www.ispub.com/journal/the-internet-journal-of-neurology/volume-9-number-1/inspiration-from-dreams-in-neuroscience-research.html#sthash.i8wM9gW0.dpuf.

14. D. Todman: "Inspiration from dreams in neuroscience research," *The Internet Journal of Neurology* 9, no. 1 (2008): 10.5580/1b79. See more at http://www.ispub.com/journal/the-internet-journal-of-neurology/volume-9-number-1/inspiration-from-dreams-in-neuroscience-research.html#sthash.i8wM9gW0.dpuf.

15. Paul Strathern, *Mendeleyev's Dream: The Quest for the Elements* (New York: Thomas Dunne Books, an imprint of St. Martin's Press, 2000), 286.

16. Pallub Ghosh, "Optical computing and the American Dream," *New Scientist*, August 18, 1988, 40; http://books.google.com/books?id=V6EzFhBqMv0C.

17. Ibid.

18. "Precognitive Dreams," Dictionary.com LLC., September 21, 2008. http://www.reference.com/browse/Precognitive_dreams.

19. Ibid.

20. "Battle of Waterloo," Dictionary.com LLC, October, 11, 2008, http://www.reference.com/browse/wiki/Battle_of_Waterloo.

21. Dee Brown, adapted for young readers by Amy Ehrlich, *Wounded Knee: An Indian History of the American West* (New York: Henry Holt and Company, 1970, 1974), 36.

22. "Abraham Lincoln: Lincoln's Dream," World History Project, USA, January 2007, http://history-world.org/lincoln.htm.

23. David Pratt, "Fate or Free Will," *Sunrise*, August/September 1998, http://www.theosophy-nw.org/theosnw/karma/ka-prat.htm.

24. Fr. Kristopher and Matushka Elizabeth Dowling, "The Real St. Patrick, Bishop of Ireland," The Celtic Orthodox Christian Church, http://celticchristianity.org/library/patrick.html.

25. Kate Clifford Larson, *Bound for the Promised Land: Harriet Tubman, Portrait of an American Hero* (New York: Ballantine Books, 2004).

26. "Strange Case of Dr Jekyll and Mr Hyde," Wikipedia, March 12, 2013, http://en.wikipedia.org/wiki/Strange_Case_of_Dr_Jekyll_and_Mr_Hyde#History.

27. "Frankenstein," Wikipedia, March 10, 2013, http://en.wikipedia.org/wiki/Frankenstein.

28. Korky Vann, "Nike: From Greek Myth to Sports and Fitness Powerhouse," http://shoes.about.com/od/athleticshoes/a/nike.htm.

29. Barry Miles, *Paul McCartney—Many Years from Now* (New York: Henry Holt, 1997), 202.

Chapter 2: A Journey into Dream Interpretation

1. Mark Prigg, "Deathbed theory dreamt by an Indian maths genius is finally proved correct—almost 100 years after he died," MailOnline, December 28,

2012, http://www.dailymail.co.uk/sciencetech/article-2254352/Deathbed-dream
-puzzles-renowned-Indian-mathematician-Srinivasa-finally-solved—100-years-
died.html#ixzz2GxOqYjEN.

Chapter 4: Common Dream Themes

1. Linda Lane Magallón, "Flying Dream FAQ," dreamflyer.net, 1999, http://
www.dreamflyer.net/flying/dreams10.html.

Chapter 5: Types of Dreams and Their Interpretations

1. Sandra Weintraub, "Cultivate Your Dreams to Find New Solutions," Winston
J. Brill & Associates, article #179 from *R&D Innovator* 4, no.10, October 1995,
http://www.winstonbrill.com/bril001/html/article_index/articles151_200.html.

Chapter 6: How to Interpret Your Dreams

1. Sandra Weintraub, *The Hidden Intelligence: Innovation through Intuition*
(Woburn, Mass.: Butterworth–Heinemann, 1998), 263.

Chapter 7: Reinterpreting Dreams

1. Kelly Bulkeley, Ph.D., "14 Weirdest Dreams in Hollywood (Kristen Bell),"
Dream Research & Education online, March 2, 2010, http://kellybulkeley.com/
14-weirdest-dreams-hollywood/2/. Used by permission.
2. Ibid.
3. "Kristen Bell," Wikipedia, March 12, 2013, http://en.wikipedia.org/wiki/
Kristen_Bell.
4. Kelly Bulkeley, Ph.D., "14 Weirdest Dreams in Hollywood (Ray Winstone),"
Dream Research & Education online, March 2, 2010, http://kellybulkeley.com/
14-weirdest-dreams-hollywood/. Used by permission.
5. Ibid.
6. Kelly Bulkeley, Ph.D., "14 Weirdest Dreams in Hollywood (Samuel L. Jackson)," Dream Research & Education online, March 2, 2010, http://kellybulkeley
.com/14-weirdest-dreams-hollywood/. Used by permission.
7. Ibid.
8. "Samuel L. Jackson," Wikipedia, March 9, 2013, http://en.wikipedia.org/wiki/
Samuel_L._Jackson; Joe Dwinell, "Brangelina take over the 'World'" *Boston Herald*
Inside Track online, September 16, 2008, http://bostonherald.com/inside_track/
celebrity_news/2008/09/brangelina_take_over_%E2%80%98world%E2%80%99.
9. Kelly Bulkeley, Ph.D., "14 Weirdest Dreams in Hollywood (Kate Winslet),"
Dream Research & Education online, March 2, 2010, http://kellybulkeley.com/
14-weirdest-dreams-hollywood/2/. Used by permission.
10. Ibid.
11. Kelly Bulkeley, Ph.D., "14 Weirdest Dreams in Hollywood (Judd Apatow),"
Dream Research & Education online, March 2, 2010, http://kellybulkeley.com/
14-weirdest-dreams-hollywood/2/. Used by permission.
12. Ibid.

13. This dream and the meaning of the key word symbols were paraphrased from Dreamcrowd online, part of the Dreamcrowd Network, http://dreamcrowd.com/dream/59853/me/1.

Chapter 8: When God Gives a Dream

1. Anita Stratos, "Egypt: Perchance to Dream: Dreams and Their Meaning in Ancient Egypt," Tour Egypt, 2012, http://www.touregypt.net/featurestories/dream.htm.

Chapter 9: How to Reawaken Your Dreams

1. James R. Lewis and Evelyn Dorothy Oliver, *The Dream Encyclopedia*, 2nd ed. (Canton, Mich.: Visible Ink Press, 2009), 181.

Cindy McGill has a passion to help people find their purpose, receive healing from life's trauma and live their lives to the fullest. She travels internationally, teaching on the subject of dreams and dream interpretation, and leads "dream teams," using innovative methods to help others discover the hidden meanings behind their dreams and give them a chance to find truth at the point of their need.

Cindy has interpreted thousands of dreams at events in the United States and abroad, including the Olympics, the Sundance Film Festival, Burning Man in the Black Rock Desert of Nevada and other expos and festivals. She has appeared on various media, including radio and TV, teaching on dreams and interpreting the dreams of others. Cindy is a keynote speaker and has also authored numerous articles for magazines and online media outlets. In 2011, she was featured in *Dreams, A Documentary*, which chronicles live dream interpretation encounters that took place at the Sundance Film Festival at Park City, Utah, and won awards at various independent film festivals around the world.

Cindy uses life-coaching skills to help people who need hope and change. She and her husband, Tim, have been successful at helping people redefine their lives and find healing and direction since 1979. They have two grown daughters and four grandchildren. Connect with Cindy at www.cindymcgill.com.

David Sluka is a writer and consultant who focuses on themes of leadership, communication and publishing. He has written for authors such as James Goll, Ed Silvoso, Patricia King, Joan Hunter, Joshua Mills, Audrey Meisner and others. Connect with David at www.david-sluka.com.